China in the Twentieth Century

Historical Association Studies
General Editors: Roger Mettam, M. E. Chamberlain and James Shields

The Historical Association, 59a Kennington Park Road, London SE11 4JH

China in the Twentieth Century

P. J. BAILEY

Basil Blackwell

30677

Copyright © P. J. Bailey

First published 1988

Basil Blackwell Ltd
108 Cowley Road, Oxford, OX4 1JF, UK

Basil Blackwell Inc.
432 Park Avenue South, Suite 1503
New York, NY 10016, USA

British Library Cataloguing in Publication Data
Bailey, Paul
    China in the twentieth century.—
    (Historical Association studies).
    1. China 1912–198/
    I. Title
    951.04

    ISBN 0–631–15448–5

Library of Congress Cataloging-in-Publication Data
Bailey, Paul, 1937–
    China in the twentieth century / Paul Bailey.
        p.   cm.—(Historial Association studies)
    Includes bibliographical references and index.
    ISBN 0–631–15448–5 (pbk.)
    1. China—History—20th century.   2.
    Communism—China—History.
I. Title.   II. Series.
DS774.B27 1988
951.04—dc19   88—10482
                                                     CIP

Typeset in 9½ on 10 pt Baskerville by Photo·Graphics, Honiton, Devon
Printed in Great Britain by Whitstable Litho Ltd., Whitstable, Kent

Contents

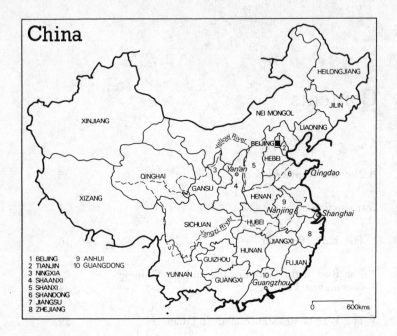

China

HEILONGJIANG
JILIN
NEI MONGOL
LIAONING
XINJIANG
Yellow River
BEIJING 1 2
HEBEI
QINGHAI
3 Yan'an
5
6 Qingdao
GANSU
4
HENAN
9
XIZANG
7
Nanjing
Shanghai
SICHUAN
Yangzi River
HUBEI
8
JIANGXI
HUNAN
GUIZHOU
FUJIAN
YUNNAN
GUANGXI
10
Guangzhou

1 BEIJING 9 ANHUI
2 TIANJIN 10 GUANGDONG
3 NINGXIA
4 SHAANXI
5 SHANXI
6 SHANDONG
7 JIANGSU
8 ZHEJIANG

0   600kms

A Note on Romanization

The text uses the *pinyin* system of romanization. Some place names, such as Beijing, will by now have become familiar to western readers while others, such as Guangzhou (Canton), will not. Also, I have retained the traditional romanization for two figures, Sun Yat-sen and Chiang Kai-shek, since their pinyin equivalents (Sun Zhongshan and Jiang Jieshi) are far less well known.

Introduction

> The whole nation is now inclined towards a republican form
> of government . . . By observing the nature of the people's
> aspirations we learn the will of Heaven . . . We recognize the
> signs of the age, and We have tested the trend of popular
> opinion; and We now, with the Emperor at our side, invest
> the nation with sovereign power, and decree the establishment
> of a constitutional government on a republican basis. (Quoted
> in Iröns, 1983, p. 35)

Thus did the Qing dynasty, which had ruled over China since 1644,
pass from the scene as the regent, the empress-dowager Longyu,
formally announced the abdication of the dynasty in February 1912
on behalf of the six-year-old emperor, Puyi. The downfall of the
dynasty had been presaged the previous October when an army
mutiny in the city of Wuchang (Hubei province) had rapidly ignited
anti-dynastic uprisings and political manoeuvres in central and
southern China. Henceforth China officially became a Republic, thus
signalling the end of an imperial tradition that dated from the third
century BC and which had ascribed enormous powers to the emperors.
Unlike the English, French and Russian revolutions, however, there
were to be no royal executions. The ex-emperor and his immediate
family were allowed to continue residing in the Forbidden City,
where the imperial palace was located, and they were to be provided
with an annual subsidy by the new republican government.

The Qing had been one of the most successful of China's dynasties.
The Qing rulers were Manchus, originally nomadic and hunting
tribes in the north-east, beyond the Great Wall. Under the able
leadership of Nurhaci (1559–1626) and his heirs, the Manchu tribes
were united and organized into a formidable military force. Abahai
(1592–1643), Nurhaci's son, began conducting raids into China. At
the same time he created a civil administration, based on Chinese
practice and employing captured Chinese, in his capital at Mukden
(present-day Shenyang). The reigning Ming dynasty (1368–1644) in
China was ill-prepared to meet the growing Manchu threat on its
north-eastern frontier. A succession of indecisive emperors, corruption

1

and factionalism within the bureaucracy, and increasing peasant unrest as a result of famine and burdensome taxes had severely weakened the dynasty. When a large-scale rebellion led by Li Zicheng resulted in the capture of Beijing in 1644 by peasant rebels and the suicide of the Ming emperor, the Manchus seized their opportunity and entered China promising to restore peace and stability. With the aid of Chinese military commanders, alarmed at the disorder and anarchy in Beijing and elsewhere, the Manchus defeated Li Zicheng and established a new dynasty, the Qing.

By insisting they were the legitimate heirs of the Ming dynasty and guaranteeing the continued status of the Chinese gentry class, the Manchus gained acceptance from the governing elite. The gentry, deriving their status from success in civil service examinations based on the Confucian classics, saw themselves as the scholarly guardians of a tradition that emphasized strict adherence to hierarchical relationships (such as that between a ruler and his subject, father and son, husband and wife) and respect for the past, one's ancestors and the elderly. Since the Qing continued the practice of recruiting officials from among the gentry, while the latter in turn were potentially a useful ally in promoting social stability, the relationship between emperor and gentry has often been described as a 'symbiotic' one. By the 1680s the Manchus had consolidated their hold over the country. Despite early attempts to maintain their Manchu identity, the Qing rulers quickly became 'Sinicized'. They not only ruled in accordance with Chinese administrative procedures, but also patronized Confucian scholarship and learning. Under three remarkable emperors, Kangxi (r. 1661–1722), Yongzheng (r. 1723–35) and Qianlong (r. 1735–96), the Qing ushered in a period of stability and economic prosperity which endured throughout most of the eighteenth century. Qing control was extended to Mongolia, Tibet and Turkestan (later to become the province of Xinjiang), while neighbouring kingdoms such as Korea, Vietnam, Nepal and Siam all acknowledged the political and cultural superiority of the Middle Kingdom (as China was known) by sending regular tributary missions to the Qing court.

By the early nineteenth century, however, there were ominous signs that the dynasty was in decline. The last years of the Qianlong reign were marked by complacency and corruption at all levels of the bureaucracy. Embezzlement of government funds destined for the upkeep of public works such as irrigation channels and dykes exacerbated the natural disasters of drought and floods to which China had always been susceptible (Wakeman, 1975, pp. 102–6; Mann Jones and Kuhn, 1978).

Furthermore, the peace and stability of the eighteenth century had led to an enormous increase in population which far outstripped the amount of cultivable land available. It is generally agreed that the population doubled during the course of the eighteenth century from approximately 150 milllion to over 350 million. By the middle of the nineteenth century China's population had reached 430 million. By way of contrast, Europe's population increased from 144 million in 1750 to 193 million in 1800 (Ping-ti Ho, 1959, p. 270; Hucker, 1975, p. 330; Gernet, 1982, p. 486). Competition for land resources often pitted immigrant Chinese settlers in violent conflict with indigenous minority peoples, particularly in the provinces of Hunan, Sichuan and Guizhou. A series of revolts broke out in the late eighteenth century and the early nineteenth century which the Manchu military forces, long accustomed to internal peace and their original martial vigour dissipated in easy living, had great difficulty in suppressing.

The dynasty's problems were compounded by the emergence of a new and far more dangerous threat, increasing aggressive demands by an expanding West for economic and trading privileges. Although Portuguese and Spanish traders had appeared off China's southern coast in the sixteenth and seventeenth centuries, it was not until the early nineteenth century that western, particularly British, traders arrived in greater numbers. In accordance with China's view of herself as the self-contained centre of the civilized world, westerners were regarded as little better than barbarians and their trading activities were restricted. Britain, emerging from the Napoleonic Wars as the most powerful western commercial and maritime power, saw herself as the champion of free trade and the upholder of an international system of equal nation states. A clash was inevitable (Hsü, 1975; Wakeman, 1975). That clash was to result in China having to sign treaties with the western powers which Chinese nationalists in the twentieth century were to condemn as 'unequal' since they were imposed upon China by force and granted the powers privileges and concessions in China which substantially infringed upon her sovereignty.

The forcible 'opening' of China began with the Opium War of 1840–2, caused by Britain's aggressive response to the dynasty's attempt to stamp out the lucrative opium trade in which British traders were engaged. The ensuing Nanjing Treaty ceded Hong Kong to Britain and opened five treaty ports for British trade and in which gunboats could be stationed. British residents in the treaty ports were to enjoy the privilege of extra-territoriality (i.e. they were subject only to the jurisdiction of the British consul) while China had to agree to a uniform, moderate tariff (whose rate was laid down by Britain) on all British imports. This latter aspect of the treaty meant that China had been compelled to sign away tariff autonomy. Similar privileges were extended to France and the United States in subsequent treaties. As a result of further hostilities with Britain and France between 1856 and 1860, the Qing court was forced to grant more concessions. Additional treaty ports were opened, the right of inland navigation was granted, missionaries were allowed to travel, preach and own land in the interior (as well as to enjoy the privilege of extra-territoriality), and permanent foreign legations were to be established in the capital.

Meanwhile the Qing dynasty had to contend with a series of internal rebellions during the mid nineteenth century, the most serious of which was the Taiping Rebellion (1850–64). The Taiping leaders forged an ideology that amalgamated Christian doctrine with traditional Chinese utopian ideals. They called for the overthrow of the corrupt Manchu dynasty and the creation of a new regime, the Taiping Tianguo (Heavenly Kingdom of Great Peace). Millions of landless peasants, and unemployed handicraft and transport workers rallied to their cause. The weakness of the dynasty was cruelly exposed. Due to the inadequacy of the Manchu military forces, the Qing were compelled to rely on regional militia armies led by the Chinese scholar–official elite to defeat the Taipings, a task they were only too willing to perform since the Taipings' anti-Confucian propaganda and egalitarian ideals threatened to undermine their own position (Kuhn, 1978). These regional militia leaders became powerful and influential provincial officials and although they remained loyal to the dynasty a fatal precedent had been set. The dynasty's ability to impose its control over the provinces was seriously impaired. Tax revenues, for example, which were meant to be passed on to the Board of Revenue in the capital were appropriated by provincial governors.

Although a 'self-strengthening movement' was promoted by the court and certain provincial officials during the 1860s and 1870s in which it was hoped the importation of western military technology would help to reinvigorate the traditional political and social order and strengthen the country against renewed western pressure, the dynasty was unable to block the West's increasing presence in China. During the turmoil of the Taiping Rebellion, foreigners had taken over administration of the maritime customs in Shanghai. This practice was then extended to the other treaty ports in the 1860s. Also, in a number of treaty ports the powers were able to demarcate 'concession' areas in which they exercised legal jurisdiction and controlled local administration (Feuerwerker, 1983b); the limitations of the self-strengthening movement were clearly shown when the Qing dynasty attempted to reassert its traditional influence in Korea and suffered a humiliating defeat in 1895 at the hands of Japan, which was bent on expanding its presence in the Korean peninsula. The treaty of Shimonoseki which ended the war conferred on Japan the same privileges previously gained by the western powers (as well as ceding Taiwan to Japan). The treaty also allowed foreigners to establish factories in the treaty ports whose products would be exempt from Chinese internal taxes.

Since the Shimonoseki treaty also saddled China with an enormous indemnity the Qing court was compelled to seek foreign loans and this, in turn, gave the powers additional influence over the Chinese government; They used this influence to gain railway and mining concessions from the late nineteenth century onwards. When, in 1897–8, the powers secured leasehold territories in which Chinese sovereignty was eliminated (e.g. Britain secured a ninety-nine-year lease on the area, to be known as the New Territories, adjoining the Kowloon peninsula), it seemed to many Chinese that the country was about to be partitioned. Fears were expressed that China would become another Poland.

For a brief period in 1898, known as the One Hundred Days, a number of Chinese scholars were able to gain influence with the Guangxu Emperor and persuade him to issue reform edicts calling for the establishment of a political advisory council, the abolition of sinecure posts in the bureaucracy, the promotion of industry and commerce, and the creation of a national school system which would include western learning in the curriculum. A hostile conservative reaction at court headed by the emperor's aunt, the empress-dowager Cixi, led to the arrest of the reformers (the two most prominent, Kang Youwei and Liang Qichao, escaped with their lives and sought refuge in Japan) and the virtual placing of Guangxu under house arrest (Kwong, 1984).

Cixi, now in control of the government, took the disastrous decision to support the xenophobia stimulated by the Boxers, a secret society active in the provinces of Zhili (present-day Hebei) and Shandong. The Boxers began by attacking western missionaries and Chinese Christians, as well as destroying railways and telegraph lines, which were associated with the hated foreigner. When they besieged the foreign legations in Beijing Cixi attempted to ride the anti-foreign wave by declaring war on the powers in 1900. It is indicative, however, of the dynasty's inability to impose its will on the whole country that the court's rash decision to wage war on the powers was not supported by provincial governors in the south, who, by guaranteeing to protect foreign lives and property in their own domains, succeeded in preventing the spread of the conflict. A nine-power expeditionary force marched on Beijing and relieved the legations. A harsh settlement was imposed on the Qing, including the payment of an indemnity and the permanent stationing of foreign troops between Beijing and Tianjin.

The dynasty's humiliation was complete. During the course of the nineteenth century the dynasty had not only been weakened by internal rebellion and its control from the centre threatened by the growing influence of powerful provincial officials and the local gentry elite, but it had also had to suffer the ignominy of defeat at the hands of foreign powers. Their presence and privileges in China had relegated her, in the later words of Mao Zedong, to the status of a 'semi-colony', well symbolized by the park sign in Shanghai's International Settlement (primarily under British control) which forbade the entrance of 'dogs and Chinese'. It is impossible to understand the Chinese revolution of the twentieth century without taking into account the humiliation felt by an entire generation of educated Chinese in the wake of this foreign presence.

Between 1901 and 1911 the empress-dowager Cixi, in a last desperate attempt to guarantee the survival of the dynasty, launched a series of political, educational and military reforms. These included the abolition of the traditional civil service examinations in 1905 and their replacement by a national system of modern schools (Borthwick, 1983); the encouragement of study abroad, particularly in Japan, which was seen as an inspiring example of an Asian country that had successfully modernized and gained respect from the western powers, especially after its defeat of Russia in 1905 in a war fought to decide which country would exert dominant influence in South Manchuria (Jansen, 1980); the adoption in 1908 of a nine year constitutional programme that would culminate in the creation of a national parliament (Fincher, 1981); and plans to form a unified and well-equipped national army (Fung, 1980).

Amidst an atmosphere of increasing nationalism, particularly amongst students, merchants, army officers and urban-based gentry, and growing hostility to the Manchu regime, these reforms back-fired (Wright, 1968; Ichiko, 1980). Chinese students who went to Japan, for example, were exposed to a wide variety of western political thought via Japanese translations. Their attraction to the concepts of nationalism and democracy made them increasingly critical of the Qing dynasty, which was blamed for China's backwardness and humiliation at the hands of the foreign powers. Initially influenced by the reformism of Kang Youwei and Liang Qichao, the two scholars who had sought exile in Japan after the abortive 1898 reforms and who advocated a constitutional monarchy (Spence, 1981), many of these students joined Sun Yat-sen's anti-Manchu organization, the Tongmenghui (Alliance League), which was founded in Tokyo in 1905.

Sun Yat-sen (1866–1925), a western-educated Chinese of peasant origin, had spent much of his early life in Hawaii and the British colony of Hong Kong (ceded by China in 1842). He founded his first anti-Manchu organization in 1894 and by 1895 was openly calling for the establishment of a republic. After an unsuccessful attempt to foment an uprising in Guangzhou in 1895 Sun spent the next sixteen years in exile. At first he concentrated on seeking support from overseas Chinese in North America and South-East Asia, as well as making contacts with traditional secret societies inside China, but after 1905 he was to gain increasing support from Chinese students and intellectuals in Japan (Schiffrin, 1968).

Sun's revolutionary platform in 1905, known later as the Three People's Principles, advocated nationalism (i.e. anti-Manchuism), democracy (i.e. the creation of a republic) and the improvement of the people's livelihood. Sun equated this last principle with socialism and claimed that by carrying out political and social revolution simultaneously China could prevent the emergence of the glaring class differences prevalent in the industrialized West. Between 1905 and 1910 a furious debate broke out between Sun and his followers on the one hand and reformers like Liang Quichao on the other, who warned of the anarchy and chaos that would result from republican revolution as well as dismissing socialism as inapplicable to China (Gasster, 1969; Young, 1970; Bernal, 1976). As hostility to the Qing dynasty grew, however, Liang's call for a constitutional monarchy became increasingly unpopular amongst radical students.

Radical students returning from Japan often took up teaching posts in the new modern schools, where they were able to spread revolutionary propaganda. One of the more celebrated was China's first modern woman revolutionary, Qiu Jin, who engaged in anti-Manchu activity while directing a local girls' school in Zhejiang province. She was arrested and executed in 1907 after being implicated in an unsuccessful uprising (Spence, 1981, pp. 50–60). Returning students were also able to infiltrate the new army units being created in China, many of whose officers had been trained in military academies in Japan, where they had come under the influence of anti-Manchu propaganda.

The Qing court, perceiving a direct connection in the West between constitutionalism and national strength, hoped that its constitutional programme would co-opt the gentry elite and thus rally support for the throne. In 1909, as part of its programme, the court sanctioned the creation of provincial assemblies, but far from playing a unifying role and encouraging loyalty to the throne they demanded greater powers and the immediate convocation of a national parliament. The assemblies, dominated by the upper stratum of the gentry elite, not only criticized the court's subservience in the wake of foreign demands for railway and mining concessions, but also grew increasingly resentful of the government's attempt to limit their role in public affairs (Fincher, 1968, 1981).

Regional studies have also shown that not only did the Qing's half-hearted attempt at constitutional reform alienate the gentry and an increasingly politicized merchant class, but also that other aspects of the court's reform programme, such as the building of modern schools, aroused popular discontent since the burden of increased taxes to pay for such measures often fell on the poorer sections of the community (Rhoads, 1975; Esherick, 1976). The last years of the Qing witnessed frequent tax revolts and modern school buildings themselves were often the target of popular wrath.

The army mutiny at Wuchang, in October 1911, was prompted by disturbances in Sichuan province where the gentry had protested violently against the dynasty's attempt to bring the provincial railway under central government control. The Wuchang mutiny was soon followed by anti-dynastic uprisings in the central and southern provinces, where the provincial assemblies, in alliance with army commanders (many of whom declared themselves as military governors), declared their independence from Beijing. The court called upon Yuan Shikai, the commander of the first modern army unit (known as the Beiyang army), to quell the uprising. Representatives of the southern provinces met in Nanjing and declared their intention to establish a republic. Sun Yat-sen, who was in the United States seeking funds at the time of the Wuchang mutiny, was elected provisional president and was given a rapturous welcome when he returned to China in December 1911.

As Yuan's government troops besieged Wuchang and a stalemate ensued between the two opposing forces, the revolutionaries sought to negotiate a deal. Sun Yat-sen offered to hand over the presidency to Yuan Shikai if he openly declared support for the republic and promised to abide by a new constitution. The revolutionaries also assumed that Yuan would be able to use his enormous power and influence to persuade the dynasty to abdicate (Young, 1968).

Some misgivings were raised about this compromise. Yuan Shikai, after all, had risen to prominence as an important military and civilian official of the Qing dynasty. He was responsible for training and commanding the first modern army unit in China, and after 1898 he was successively governor of Shandong province and governor-general of Zhili province as well as being a member of the Grand Council in Beijing (MacKinnon, 1980). It was also widely believed that Yuan had broken a promise of support for the 1898 reformers in backing Cixi's coup against the Guangxu emperor and his advisers. Following Cixi's death in 1908 jealousy of Yuan's influence resulted in his forced retirement. After the Wuchang uprising Yuan was recalled to command the government forces and appointed prime minister of a cabinet that had been formed as part of the dynasty's constitutional reform programme.

Recognition of the fact that Yuan had the most modern and well-equipped military force at his disposal and the real fear held by revolutionaries that continued civil war might prompt the intervention of the powers to protect their economic stake in China convinced them, however, that a compromise was necessary. Yuan, for his part, was well aware that support for the dynasty was crumbling as some provinces in the north in November 1911 joined the south in declaring

8

independence from Beijing. In February 1912 he secured the dynasty's abdication and the following month Sun Yat-sen handed over the provisional presidency to Yuan Shikai. Although the revolutionaries had hoped the capital would be located in Nanjing, Yuan was able to get his own way and have the capital in Beijing, the centre of his military power.

The 1911 revolution, therefore, had been spearheaded by provincial assemblies (dominated by the upper gentry elite) and army commanders who declared themselves provincial military governors. It had resulted in the accession to power of someone very much associated with the old regime whose commitment to a republic was ambiguous. Sun Yat-sen's revolutionary organization, the Tong-menghui, although it had been instrumental in spreading anti-Manchu and republican propaganda amongst students and new army units, had played a minor role in the events of 1911–12. Nevertheless, hopes were high that the creation of a republic would usher in a new era for China, one in which she would gain the respect of the foreign powers and lay the foundations for a democratic and prosperous nation. The events of the following decade would result in the crushing of those hopes and the emergence of radical new solutions to deal with the political and economic problems that continued to plague China.

1 The Early Republic

Yuan Shikai (1859–1916) has been traditionally condemned by historians as an unprincipled opportunist who showed little understanding of, or commitment to, republican government (Ch'en, 1961). He was ultimately to betray the Republic by attempting to restore the monarchy in 1915 with himself as emperor. Recent studies by Young (1976, 1977, 1983) modify this view by portraying Yuan as a 'modernizing conservative' who made an unsuccessful bid to reassert centralized control and thus reverse the trend towards regionalism that had emerged during the last years of the Qing dynasty. While on the one hand Yuan's freedom of manoeuvre was restricted by increasing foreign influence over the economy – Young (1977, p. 4) compares China during this period with a Third World nation struggling for autonomy – his centralizing policies, on the other hand, aroused the opposition of both provincial military governors and local gentry and merchant elites. Other studies of this period, however, have focused on the activities of the political parties, whose corruption and factionalism during the early Republic did as much as Yuan's policies to bring republican government into disrepute (Yu, 1966; Nathan, 1976).

Politics in the Early Republic

Most observers in 1912 assumed that Yuan would abide by constitutional procedures. Under the provisional constitution approved in early 1912 Yuan Shikai, as president, had considerable executive power but was also to share responsibility with a prime minister (whom the president was to appoint with the concurrence of parliament) and his cabinet. Elections were also to be held at the end of 1912 and the beginning of 1913 for a bicameral parliament and new provincial assemblies, to replace the old National Assembly and provincial assemblies that had been convened during the last years of the Qing dynasty.

Sun Yat-sen's pre-1911 revolutionary organization, the Tongmenghui, was now reorganized into a parliamentary political party, the Guomindang (nationalist party), to contest the elections promised for the end of the year. Other political parties were formed, whose membership included officials and bureaucrats associated with the *ancien régime* as well as former revolutionaries. Alliances among them were made and unmade with bewildering frequency, and their factionalism and susceptibility to government bribes were severely to damage the credibility of parliamentary politics.

With the effective organizational skills of Song Jiacren, an associate of Sun Yat-sen, the Guomindang, in contrast to the other parties, embarked on a well-planned and co-ordinated electoral campaign (Liew, 1971). The party called for local self-government as well as limited presidential power and cabinet responsibility to parliament. The elections, in which between 4 and 6 per cent of the population were entitled to vote, were a victory for the Guomindang, which emerged as the largest single party in both houses of parliament (Fincher, 1981; Young, 1983). The military governors of Anhui, Jiangxi and Guandong provinces were also adherents of the Guomindang. Yuan Shikai regarded the election results as a threat to his own position. It was no coincidence that in March 1913, a month before the parliament was due to meet, Song Jiaoren, who, more than anyone, had spearheaded the campaign for a cabinet system of government and ministerial responsibility to parliament, was assassinated in Shanghai. It was widely believed that Song's murder had been carried out on Yuan's orders.

Yuan's already strained relations with the Guomindang reached a crisis point in April 1913 over the question of foreign loans. Yuan had been hampered from the beginning of his presidency by a lack of funds. By 1911 the central government derived most of its revenue from the maritime customs duties, since a large proportion of the land tax and other internal taxes had been appropriated by the provinces. During the course of the revolution the foreign powers tightened their control over the maritime customs by taking over the collection, banking and remittance of customs revenue. Such revenue was to be deposited in foreign banks and then remitted to the Chinese government specifically for the repayment of foreign loans contracted by the former regime (Feuerwerker, 1983b).

The customs revenue was also to be pledged for foreign loans contracted after 1912; such loans, however, had to be negotiated through a six-power Banking Consortium representing Britain, the United States, France, Germany, Russia and Japan. This Consortium, originally created in 1910, effectively blocked any attempt by Yuan's government to negotiate with individual foreign banks. Yuan, anxious to secure funds and formal recognition of his regime by the powers, obtained a Re-organization Loan of £25 million from the Consortium in April 1913. Of this sum Yuan was actually to receive £21 million since the loan was to comprise bonds sold at only 90 per cent of their face value, with a further 6 per cent of the total deducted for

11

commission. The original principal, however, at 5 per cent interest, still had to be repaid (Mancall, 1984, p. 200). The salt-tax revenue was pledged as security for the loan and in order to ensure its efficient collection foreigners were to assist in the salt-tax administration (Feuerwerker, 1983b). Foreign influence over the economy was thus further expanded. (The United States, under the presidency of Woodrow Wilson, hoping to dissociate itself from this infringement of Chinese sovereignty, withdrew from the Consortium. Any Chinese hopes, however, that the United States would henceforth champion China's cause were to remain largely unfulfilled.) As further testimony to the weakness of the new Republic, Yuan was compelled in 1913 formally to recognize the autonomy of Outer Mongolia and Tibet (which were originally part of the Qing empire but had now broken loose from Beijing's control during the 1911 Revolution) before Russia and Britain, who had strategic interests in those areas, would formally recognize Yuan's regime.

Since Yuan had signed the Re-organization Loan without consulting parliament, the Guomindang attempted to impeach the president. Yuan averted this threat, primarily through manipulation of the other political parties, and then went on to the offensive. He dismissed the Guomindang military governors of Jiangxi, Anhui and Guangdong provinces and replaced them with his own nominees. Armed conflict broke out in the south (to be known as the Second Revolution) as the dismissed governors and their Guomindang followers sought to launch a nationwide campaign against Yuan.

The Second Revolution barely lasted three months (July to September 1913) and ended in a complete rout of the anti-Yuan forces. Yuan's ability to buy the support of important provincial military governors, in addition to the general antipathy felt by the gentry and merchant elites for the disruptive influence of the Guomindang, ensured the defeat of the uprising. Sun Yat-sen, bitterly disillusioned, was forced once more to go into exile. He went to Japan, where he founded a new party, the Chinese Revolutionary Party (Zhonghua Gemingdang), which represented a reaction against the broad-based and open parliamentary party that had been the Guomindang in 1912 (Friedman, 1974). Sun now emphasized the importance of a tightly-knit secret party organization, whose members would swear an oath of loyalty to him personally.

Yuan's victory enabled him to expand his control in the provinces as well as to launch a frontal assault on all self-governmment institutions. He first succeeded in coercing parliament to elect him permanent president in October 1913. By the beginning of 1914 he had banned the Guomindang and dissolved parliament. Provincial and district assemblies were also abolished. Yuan also attempted to increase Beijing's control over the provinces by appointing civilian governors to balance the power of the military governors (tutu). After

1913 he succeeded in appropriating for the central government a larger proportion of the land tax.

Young has described Yuan's regime after 1913 as a 'republican dictatorship . . . constructed around the principles of administrative centralisation and bureaucratic order' (1983, p. 238). As part of his campaign to ensure public order, Yuan ordered that primary schools, the number of which greatly increased during this period, restore the Confucian classics to the curriculum (they had been eliminated from the curriculum in 1912). The inculcation of traditional moral values such as loyalty would, it was hoped, result in the creation of a law-abiding and submissive population. It is perhaps for this reason that during Yuan's rule government expenditure on primary education was increased, often at the expense of higher education.

Yuan's policies, however, met with increasing opposition, not only from provincial military governors, but also from gentry and merchant groups (the very people, ironically, who had supported him in 1913), which resented the abolition of local assemblies, the restrictions placed on the Chambers of Commerce, and the plans to impose a government income tax. In a desperate attempt to divert opposition to his regime Yuan Shikai played his last trump card. In 1915 he encouraged a campaign calling for the restoration of the monarchy. The campaign, orchestrated by Yuan's followers, naturally led to pleas by 'concerned citizens' for Yuan to assume the Dragon Throne. Yuan, however, had committed a fatal blunder. He had assumed that the very symbols of monarchical power would be sufficient to cement national unity and enhance his personal power. The clock, however, could not be turned back. The monarchy had been totally discredited in 1911, while the military governors were too jealous of their own recently acquired power to accept the claims of a new emperor.

As Yuan prepared to install himself as emperor at the end of 1915, military governors in the south rose up in revolt. They declared their provinces independent of Beijing and prepared to launch a military campaign. At the same time Sun Yat-sen, financed by the Japanese, attempted to stage uprisings in the province of Shandong. His close association with the Japanese (and reports that he had offered Japan future economic concessions in return for her assistance) at a time when there was much anti-Japanese feeling in the country due to Japan's increasingly aggressive activity in China (see next section) laid him open to the charge of being a traitor in the pay of a foreign enemy (Friedman, 1974). Sun's campaign quickly fizzled out. As in 1911–12 it was to be the provincial military governors, and not Sun Yat-sen, who would reap the benefits of successful revolt.

Fearing the consequences of civil war, the powers were decidedly lukewarm to Yuan's scheme. Japan, in particular, was hostile and even managed to persuade Britain and the United States to submit a joint note advising postponement of the restoration. Even after Yuan abandoned his scheme in March 1916, provinces continued to declare their independence. It was only his death in June of that year which saved Yuan from the ignominy of being overthrown. Yuan's innate conservatism, his lack of sympathy for the principles of constitutional government, his ruthless treatment of political opponents and his cynical manipulation of parliament had dealt a blow to the Republic from which it was never really to recover. After 1916 a powerless parliament and a weak civilian government were increasingly to become the mere playthings of a succession of warlord factions.

China and the First World War

Before discussing the emergence of warlordism following the death of Yuan Shikai, it is necessary first of all to describe how the First World War affected China. This was a crucial phase in Chinese history, since the actions taken by Japan, Britain, the United States and France were to confirm China's weakness when confronted with the interests and ambitions of the powers themselves. The anger and disillusion which followed were to deepen a fierce nationalism, whose origins dated from the last years of the Qing dynasty.

When war broke out in Europe in August 1914, the Japanese government immediately expressed willingness to come to the aid of its ally, Britain. Under the terms of the 1902 Anglo-Japanese alliance, Japan offered to declare war on Germany. This would have given Japan the justification to attack Germany's leased territory in China (obtained in 1898), which was centred on the port of Qingdao in Shandong province. While the British government was amenable to the idea of the Japanese navy patrolling East-Asian waters to protect British shipping and trade against possible German attack it was more ambivalent about the prospect of seeing a greater Japanese presence in China. Japan's victory over Russia in 1905 had already led to an expansion of her economic influence in Manchuria (which included control of the South Manchuria Railway) and Britain, as the power still with the greatest economic stake in China, was beginning to view Japan as a potential rival.

Japan, however, went ahead with her attack on the German leased territory. Ignoring China's declaration of neutrality, Japanese troops landed in north Shandong and took Qingdao overland. In addition to Qingdao, Germany had also in 1898 obtained control of the main provincial railway from Qingdao to Jinan, the provincial capital, as well as mining concessions along the route of the railway. Despite China's attempt to limit Japan's actions, Japanese troops soon advanced inland from Qingdao and took control of the railway.

It was at this point that the Japanese government decided to

14

consolidate and strengthen her position in China by imposing on Yuan Shikai the infamous 'Twenty-One Demands'. In January 1915 the Japanese minister to China handed over to Yuan a series of demands which, if accepted in their entirety, would have virtually made China into a Japanese protectorate. These demands included not only an extension of Japan's lease of Port Arthur (in Manchuria) and the South Manchuria railway but also the granting of mining, trading and residential privileges in South Manchuria and Inner Mongolia, recognition of her dominant presence in Shangdong, and a promise by the Chinese government not to allow any part of China's coast to fall under the influence of another power. The last series of demands, however, was especially ambitious. The Chinese government was to employ Japanese political and military advisers; a joint Sino-Japanese police force was to be created; and China was to purchase a fixed amount of weapons from Japan (Chi, 1970, p. 32). Yuan Shikai prevaricated, hoping for support from Britain and the United States. Although they protested against the last series of demands, prompting Japan to agree to their 'postponement', neither Britain nor the United States was willing to antagonize Japan. Moreover, the American Secretary of State, William Jennings Bryan publicly stated in March 1915 that 'territorial contiguity' created special relations between Japan and the Chinese territories of Shandong and South Manchuria.

On 25 May 1915, a day later to be called National Humiliation Day by Chinese students, Yuan signed Japan's demands. Widespread anti-Japanese demonstrations, which often took the form of boycotts against Japanese goods, occurred in all the main cities. Despite an ineffective warning by the United States government that it would not recognize any Sino-Japanese agreement which impaired China's political and territorial integrity, Japan was able to gain approval from Britain and France in 1917 concerning her claims in Shandong, while in the same year the United States again recognized that Japan had special interests in China due to the geographical closeness of the two countries (Chi, 1970, p. 110).

Confident now that her claims in Shandong would be recognized in any future peace conference, Japan agreed to go along with Britain's attempt to persuade China to declare war on Germany. In fact, Yuan Shikai had offered in 1914 and 1915 to enter the war on the allied side (even proposing a Chinese expedition to the Dardanelles) in the hope of pre-empting Japanese military action against Germany in Shandong. For this very reason Japan had opposed the idea. Britain's motive for wanting China to declare war on Germany was simply that German property and merchant shipping in China could be requisitioned.

Duan Qirui, who had been one of Yuan Shikai's generals and who dominated the civilian cabinet in Beijing, was a keen supporter of the allied proposal. Others feared, however, that if China entered the war, Duan would secure allied funds which he could then use to strengthen his position *vis-à-vis* internal opponents. Duan intimidated the parliament, restored after Yuan Shikai's death, with a show of military force and war was declared on Germany in August 1917. The Guomindang, under Sun Yat-sen's leadership, left Beijing in protest and set up a rival parliament in Guangzhou. Henceforth Sun Yat-sen disputed the legitimacy of the Beijing government and aimed to create his own government in the South. Those who supported China's declaration of war against Germany hoped that this would not only ensure China's participation in the peace conference but would lend weight to China's demands that the unequal treaty system be ended. Although China did not participate militarily in the war, Chinese labourers were recruited by Britain and France to work in France (Summerskill, 1982). In fact, France had begun to recruit Chinese labour as early as 1916. During the next two years over 150,000 Chinese labourers went to France, where they buried war-dead, rebuilt trenches and roads, and worked in armaments and machinery works.

Chinese hopes of an end to the unequal treaty system were also given a boost by the inspiring rhetoric of President Woodrow Wilson. He talked of creating a new international system after the war, based on open diplomacy and equality of nations, as well as advocating the cause of self-determination for peoples. The Versailles Peace Conference in 1919 was to prove a bitter disappointment as Wilson's lofty ideals had to come to terms with the concrete reality of power interests. If Chinese representatives had to accept that the powers would not end extra-territoriality in China or allow her to regain tariff autonomy, they at least expected that the leased territory of Qingdao and the Jinan-Qingdao railway would be returned to Chinese control.

Japan, however, was able to bolster her claims in Shandong by referring not only to the approval given by Britain and France in 1917, but also to joint-defence treaties signed between Tokyo and Duan Qirui's government in 1918 which had implicitly recognized the Japanese presence in Shandong. More importantly, Britain and the United States, as in 1915, were not willing fully to commit themselves to China's cause and thus risk incurring the hostility of Japan, now a major military and naval power in East Asia. Furthermore, President Wilson was anxious that all the allied powers participate in the League of Nations and when Japan hinted that she might not join, Wilson bowed to the inevitable.

When news was received in China on 4 May 1919 that the allies had decided to award Germany's rights in Shandong to Japan, there were massive student demonstrations in Beijing that quickly spread to other major cities (Chow, 1960). Pro-Japanese ministers were attacked and a boycott of Japanese goods organized, in which

16

merchants and urban workers, particularly in Shanghai, participated (Chen, 1971). Chinese representatives at Versailles, bombarded by telegrams from China denouncing the peace settlement, did not sign the treaty. For the first time large numbers of students, merchants and urban workers, increasingly concerned with the fate of the nation, had been galvanised into political action. The political demonstrations which began in May 1919, however, were part of a wider process which came to be known as the May Fourth Movement.

The May Fourth Movement

In 1915 a new journal began publication in Shanghai. Entitled *Xin Qingnian* (New Youth) and edited by Chen Duxiu (1880–1942), who had studied in Japan before 1911 and participated in the 1911 revolution, the journal denounced traditional morality and practices and advocated wholesale cultural and intellectual change. For many Chinese intellectuals the corruption of republican politics had shown that changes in attitudes had to precede political change (Grieder, 1981). Chen, in particular, launched a fierce attack on Chinese tradition, arguing that the persistence of Confucian beliefs stifled the emergence of a young and dynamic citizenry. He especially criticized the traditional family system, with its emphasis on respect for the old and the relegation of women to an inferior status. The attack on Confucianism that Chen encouraged was well summed up in a popular slogan of the time: 'overthrow Confucius and sons'. Chen advocated wholesale westernization and promoted the cause of democracy and science. Chen's frontal assault on Chinese tradition *in toto* has been described as 'totalistic iconoclasm' (Lin, 1979), although a recent study has argued that Chen was able to draw on an indigenous tradition of dissent and that his radical criticisms of Chinese culture were consistently prompted by a deeply felt nationalism, in evidence since his student days during the last years of the Qing dynasty (Feigon, 1983).

Another contributor to *Xin Qingnian* was Hu Shi (1891–1962). Hu had received a government scholarship to study in the United States in 1908 and while at Cornell University he had written articles condemning the rigidity and formalism of the Chinese classical language (*wenyan*). On his return in 1917 he contributed an article to *Xin Qingnian* promoting a literature based on vernacular speech (*baihua*). Such a literature, Hu argued, would not only be more lively and practical, but would also enable China to escape the stultifying effects of Confucian culture so much associated with the classical language (Grieder, 1970). Literature was also seen as a vehicle for change by Lu Xun (1881–1936), China's foremost writer of the twentieth century. He had originally gone to Japan in the early years of the century to study medicine but had given up in despair,

17

concluding that until a fundamental change in mentality occurred amongst the people science would not of itself 'save' China. Through the medium of literature Lu Xun hoped to draw attention to the evils of traditional society and thereby encourage his compatriots to question the attitudes that underlay them (Lyell, 1976; Spence, 1981, pp. 61–71, 85–88, 107–113; Lee, 1986). In 1918 *Xin Qingnian* published his short story, 'Diary of a Madman', one of the first to be written in the vernacular, in which Lu Xun described Chinese tradition in terms of a voracious cannibalism.

The intellectual ferment created by *Xin Qingnian* and an increasing number of other journals founded at this time has led some historians to compare the May Fourth Movement with the European Enlightenment (Schwarcz, 1986), and one writer has claimed that, just as Voltaire paved the way for the French Revolution, so the May Fourth intellectuals, with their questioning of tradition and promotion of science and democracy, paved the way for the communist revolution of 1949 (Bianco, 1971, pp. 27–8). The advocacy of wholesale westernization by Chen Duxiu and Hu Shi stimulated a keen interest in western literature and political thought amongst Chinese radical youth. Writers such as Ibsen, Turgenev and Shaw were translated; in 1919 and 1920 Bertrand Russell and the American philosopher and educator John Dewey were invited to China where they lectured to rapt audiences of Chinese university students.

By 1918 Chen Duxiu, Hu Shi and Lu Xun were all teaching at Beijing University, which, under the chancellorship of Cai Yuanpei (1868–1940), had become a dynamic centre of intellectual debate. Cai, holder of the traditional metropolitan civil service degree, had joined Sun Yat-sen's Tongmenghui during the last years of the dynasty. In 1912 he became the first minister of education under the Republic but had soon resigned in protest against the policies of Yuan Shikai. In 1916 he was appointed chancellor of Beijing University where he changed its former reputation of being a haven for the sons of bureaucrats by transforming the university into a reputable academic institution. He encouraged a wide variety of views among the academic staff, insisting that the university be a place where opposing ideas and opinions could be expressed (Duiker, 1977). While teaching at the university Chen Duxiu and the others had an enormous impact on the students; Chen's relationship with his students, in fact, often took the form of the traditional Confucian teacher–pupil relationship (Feigon, 1983). Another important teacher at Beijing University was Li Dazhao (1888–1927), one of the first Chinese intellectuals to write about the Bolshevik Revolution in 1917 (Meisner, 1967). In addition to teaching in the political science department, Li was in charge of the university library. One of his assistants was Mao Zedong (1893–1976), who had come to Beijing in 1918 after graduating from normal school in his home province of Hunan. Like many students of the time, Mao was attracted to a wide variety of ideas and political thought. He admitted that on the eve of his departure for Beijing in 1918 his ideas comprised a 'curious mixture of liberalism, democratic reformism and utopian socialism' (Schram, 1966. p. 44); while in Beijing, under the influence of Li Dazhao, he was to become interested in Marxism.

It was Li Dazhao's 1918 article on the Bolshevik Revolution (published in *Xin Qingnian*) which first underlined its messianic message. For Li, the Bolshevik Revolution, as the most important event in world history, held out the hope that China, too, might emerge from a period of decay and achieve a spiritual rebirth (Meisner, 1967; Schwartz, 1979). With the creation of the Society for the Study of Marxism at Beijing University in the same year Li began to probe deeper into the doctrinal aspects of the Bolshevik Revolution. A special issue of *Xin Qingnian* in May 1919 was devoted to Marxism. It should be noted in this context that while parts of the Communist Manifesto had been translated into Chinese as early as 1906 it was not until after 1919 that a substantial number of Marxist works became available in Chinese.

Chen Duxiu also began to devote more attention to Marxism after 1919. Increasingly disappointed with republican politics in China, Chen, who had previously pinned his hopes on cultural and educational change and the gradual implementation of democracy on the Anglo-American model, argued that thorough-going social and economic transformation was needed. By 1920 he announced his conversion to Marxism. The stance taken by Chen and Li signified a breakdown in the consensus amongst May Fourth radical intellectuals, illustrated in the exchange of views between Li and Hu Shi in 1919. Hu Shi, influenced by the pragmatism of John Dewey, argued for piecemeal change and warned against the wholesale adoption of any particular ideology. In 1920 Hu Shi left the editorial group of *Xin Qingnian* and the magazine henceforth became the sounding board for the Marxist views of Chen and Li.

Disillusionment with the West as a result of the Versailles decision in 1919, and the declarations by the new Soviet government in 1918 and 1919 that it would renounce the unequal treaties concluded by Tsarist Russia and China during the nineteenth century, prompted increasing numbers of students to take an interest in Marxism. While representing to many the very latest in western thought, it was at the same time a critique of western society which spelled out a programme of action to deal with China's predicament. For others, however, disillusionment with the West prompted a rejection of western culture altogether. Liang Shuming, who taught philosophy at Beijing University, condemned the selfish individualism of western material civilization and championed a return to the spiritual values of traditional Chinese culture, values which he saw as encouraging harmony and co-operation instead of competition and greed (Alitto, 1979).

In 1919 and 1920 Marxist study groups were formed in Beijing and other cities, which loosely brought together students and intellectuals interested in radical political and economic change. The fluidity of their views, however, is illustrated by the fact that many of them also professed an interest in socialism and anarchism. In 1920 a representative from the Comintern, Voitinsky, arrived in China and met with Li Dazhao and Chen Duxiu to discuss the possibility of organizing a communist party. By early 1921 communist party branches had been set up in six cities, including Beijing, Guangzhou, Shanghai and Changsha, where Mao Zedong was particularly active. The first congress of what was to become known as the Chinese Communist Party (CCP) met in Shanghai in the summer of 1921. Twelve delegates attended (including Mao Zedong), representing perhaps no more than fifty committed communists (Harrison, 1972, pp. 31–2); Chen Duxiu, who was in Guangzhou at the time, was elected secretary-general of the new party. From these humble beginnings, the CCP, comprising initially a small number of urban-based intellectuals, was to develop rapidly in the ensuing years.

The Warlord Period, 1916–28

Although an appearance of normality was restored after Yuan Shikai's death in 1916, with the return of parliament and the succession to the presidency of the former vice-president Li Yuanhong, centralized control from Beijing, already weakened during the last year of Yuan's rule, rapidly disintegrated as provincial and local militarists strengthened their control over their respective domains (Sheridan, 1983). These militarists, or warlords as historians have come to call them, exercised direct political power, retaining control over civil administration (as well as issuing their own currency) and imposing their own taxes to pay for their armies, which were the sole basis of their power. The fiction of a civilian government in Beijing was preserved by whichever warlord faction, or clique, happened to hold sway in the north since the powers continued to recognize the Beijing government as the sole legitimate government of China. In this way the warlord faction in control of Beijing could hope to acquire legitimacy as well as the customs revenue remitted to the central government by the powers.

China was not to experience a semblance of unity until 1928 when the Guomindang established a new national government at Nanjing, but even then its control over large areas of China remained severely limited by the continued existence of former warlords, who, while acknowledging the Nanjing government, retained control of their armies (see next chapter). This has led Sheridan (1977) to describe the entire republican period from 1912 to 1949 as one in which China as a national entity became progressively fragmented, although he does make a distinction between the 1916–28 period, as one of 'pure warlordism', and that after 1928, which was one of 'residual warlordism' (1966, 1983). The 'disintegration' that Sheridan sees as characterizing the whole republican period is regarded as inevitable by Sutton, whose study of one particular army, the Yunnan Army, attempts to show that its deterioration as a united, coherent and well-motivated unit was caused by factors that equally undermined all political organizations after 1912 – the existence of an ideological vacuum following the collapse of the monarchy and the growth of provincial sentiment (Sutton, 1980).

Although several conferences were convened in the years immediately following Yuan's death to work out some form of unity amongst the warlords, the creation of various factions, or cliques, bred mutual suspicion which, after 1920, led to a series of wars that affected large areas of China (Ch'i, 1976). Such cliques were held together principally by self-interest, so that betrayals and defections were common. No one clique was able to dominate, as alliances would be formed against any that threatened to upset the status quo. This has prompted Ch'i Hsi-sheng (1976) to describe the warlord period in terms of an 'international system' in which a balance of power was the operative principle. Mancall (1984, pp. 202–3) has even likened the warlord period to Renaissance Europe, when individual states shared a common upper-class culture and the ideal of a 'universal ruler' was preserved. Another study of the warlord period, perhaps overlooking the chaos and destruction in its obsession with applying a coherent political science 'model', describes it as a time when a more openly competitive and pluralist system prevailed, in contrast to the imperial monarchy before 1911 and the totalitarian communist regime after 1949 (Pye, 1971).

While warlords frequently announced their commitment to national unity, none was willing to abandon control over his own army. The number of men under arms increased from 500,000 in 1916 to 2 million in 1928 (Ch'i 1976, p. 78) and the funds needed by warlords to retain the loyalty of their troops led them to impose a bewildering array of taxes on the hapless peasantry. Regular taxes, such as the land tax, were constantly increased and, in many cases, collected years in advance. Warlord armies themselves, recruited from among ex-bandits, the unemployed and landless peasants, wreaked havoc on local communities by engaging in systematic looting, with the result that in the popular mind there was little distinction to be made between soldiers and bandits (Lary, 1985).

While it is recognized that generally the warlord period brought misery and chaos to China, individual studies of warlords have attempted to provide a more in-depth analysis of their background and aims (Sheridan, 1966; Gillin, 1967; McCormack, 1977; Wou, 1978). Many of them came from modest backgrounds with little or no traditional education. Zhang Zuolin, the warlord of Manchuria, had been a bandit during the last years of the dynasty (McCormack, 1977); some, like Yan Xishan, the warlord of Shanxi, had received training in military academies in China and Japan (Gillin, 1967); others, like Feng Yuxiang, had risen through the ranks in one of the new army divisions created by the Qing after 1900. Some warlords, like Wu Peifu, propagated traditional Confucian values, hoping thereby to supplement their military control with moral control (Wou, 1978). Feng Yuxiang even adopted Christianity in 1914 and was one of the few warlords who systematically attempted to indoctrinate his troops with a blend of Christian maxims and Confucian homilies (Sheridan, 1966).

Very few warlords either had the inclination or the time to concentrate on political reform or economic development. Feng Yuxiang, for example, although at times showing an interest in solving such social problems as opium-smoking, was never in one place long enough to see through any changes (Sheridan, 1966). One exception was Yan Xishan, who became military governor of Shanxi in 1912 and remained in control of the province virtually until the communist victory in 1949. Yan attempted to promote both heavy and light industry, cracked down on opium-smoking and gambling, sponsored vocational education, and began to overhaul local adminis-tration by providing for village deliberative assemblies and the training of a more efficient and indoctrinated district magistracy to combat the influence of powerful local gentry (Gillin, 1967). Gillin (1967, p. 295) thinks that Yan's schemes 'constitute one of the last systematic attempts made in China to bring about reform along conservative lines'. Be that as it may, the results of his economic schemes were meagre at best, while his attempts at local government reform were consistently sabotaged by local gentry. Yan's failure to extend his control to the grass-roots level anticipated that of Chiang Kai-shek after 1928.

Before the rise of the Guomindang government in Guangzhou (see next chapter) only Feng Yuxiang, who did receive a certain amount of aid from the Soviet Union while based in the north-west, openly attacked imperialism in China, although a study of Zhang Zuolin has shown that he attempted to halt Japanese economic penetration of Manchuria by encouraging Chinese development in the region (McCormack, 1977). In the confusing and unpredictable situation that prevailed in China from 1916 onwards, foreign governments were reluctant to pin all their hopes on any one particular warlord, although most warlords were able to obtain their arms from a variety of western sources (Ch'i, 1976; Chan, 1982).

22

By 1926 a relatively stable balance of power had been created between Zhang Zuolin, who controlled the Beijing area and the north-east, and Wu Peifu, who controlled much of central China. This balance was to be upset by a revitalized Guomindang regime in Guangzhou, increasingly viewed with alarm by the foreign powers, which sought to change the rules of the game and restore China as a unified nation state.

2 The Rise of the Guomindang and the Chinese Communist Party

The emergence of the Chinese Communist Party in 1921 and the re-organization of the Guomindang between 1923 and 1926 into a highly organized and disciplined political and military force introduced radical new elements into the Chinese scene. Both parties set themselves the task of overcoming the twin evils of warlordism and imperialism, and it was on this basis that a policy of joint collaboration was implemented.

The First United Front

The first congress of the CCP in 1921, after much heated discussion, adopted an uncompromising stance towards other political organizations, including the Guomindang. In contrast to the loosely organized socialist and Marxist study groups formed in 1919 and 1920, the new party began the process of laying down strict organizational rules and membership requirements. Anarchists, for example, were excluded. Since the delegates adopted both the orthodox Marxist view that revolution would occur amongst the urban proletariat and the Leninist assumption that the party was the vanguard of the proletariat, priority was assigned to organizing urban labour with the aim of overthrowing 'the capitalist classes and all private ownership' (Harrison, 1972, p. 34), although the question of whether to join the Moscow-based Communist International (Comintern) was not raised (Schwartz, 1979, p. 34).

The reality of China's situation, however, belied the optimistic faith of early communist leaders in promoting urban revolution. Although a proletariat had begun to emerge during the last years of the Qing dynasty, principally associated with foreign factories and a smaller number of Chinese enterprises in the treaty ports, China was still overwhemingly rural in 1921. Despite the sharp increase in the number of modern Chinese enterprises, particularly in the textile industry, during and just after the First World War, as the attention of the powers elsewhere allowed more scope for native industry to develop (Feuerwerker, 1968, 1983a), there were still only just under 1.5 million Chinese workers involved in large- and medium-scale production in 1919, less than 1 per cent of the total population (Chesneaux, 1968, pp. 41, 47). This proletariat was heavily concentrated in a few large cities, particularly Shanghai.

To this figure should be added a further 12–14 million workers involved in mining, utilities, construction and handicrafts (Harrison, 1972, p. 9), most of which Chesneaux (1968) excludes from his definition of a modern proletariat because they were still enmeshed in pre-industrial labour organizations such as traditional guilds, regional associations and labour contract gangs. Yet even modern factory workers were often recruited by traditional-style labour bosses or contractors and since many of them were rural migrants who would return to their home areas during the busy harvest season, there was a high turnover of personnel.

In the 1920s only 6 per cent of China's population lived in cities of more than 50,000 and another 6 per cent in towns of between 10,000 and 50,000 (Harrison, 1972, p. 9). As late as 1933, out of a total working population of nearly 260 million, 250 million were engaged in agriculture. In 1933 agriculture contributed 65 per cent of the net domestic product, while the output of factories, handicrafts, mining and utilities constituted 10.5 per cent of the net domestic product. Within this latter category, however, modern factory production was overshadowed by handicraft manufacturing. Modern industry, in fact, accounted for only 2.2 per cent of the net domestic product in 1933 (Feuerwerker, 1968, pp. 6, 8, 10, 17). In the words of Feuerwerker (1968, p. 10), the structure of China's mainland economy before 1949 was typical of a 'pre-industrial society'.

The first congress of the CCP, nevertheless, created a Labour Secretariat in Shanghai with branches in other major cities. Between 1921 and 1923 communist activists were involved in the launching of a number of strikes for improved conditions, including a strike by Hong Kong and Guangzhou seamen in 1922. In that year a General Labour Union was formed under communist auspices, claiming to represent 100 trade unions and up to 300,000 workers (Harrison, 1972, p. 36). Recent studies have also highlighted the role played by Mao Zedong in the labour movement during these years in his home province of Hunan (MacDonald, 1978; Shaffer, 1982), in contrast to the standard English-language biographies of Mao (Ch'en, 1965; Schram, 1966), which tend to gloss over this period of his revolutionary career.

In 1921 Mao became head of the Hunan branch of the Labour Secretariat and during the next two years helped to organize successful strikes amongst miners, construction workers and printers, many of whom belonged to traditional guilds and hence were not included in Chesneaux's definition of a modern working class. Despite Shaffer's (1982) contention that the trade unions in Hunan were well organized and acquired a large following, in contrast to the view taken by MacDonald (1978) that the labour movement in Hunan was always dependent on urban elite support, many of these unions were ultimately closed down by the authorities. The vulnerability of the labour movement nationwide was made painfully obvious in early 1923 when the warlord Wu Peifu, whom many had seen as a reformer, brutally suppressed the Beijing–Hankou railway workers' strike.

Meanwhile the CCP came under increasing pressure from the Comintern to form an alliance with the Guomindang. In a 1920 speech to the Second Congress of the Comintern, known as the Theses on the National and Colonial Questions, Lenin had argued that the newly founded communist parties in the colonial world (in particular Asia) needed to co-operate initially with the more powerful bourgeois nationalist parties or groups, who shared common aims of national unification and freedom from foreign control and exploitation. The Comintern, in fact, at first looked to warlords such as Wu Peifu as potential allies but finally decided on the Guomindang as a suitable candidate with which the CCP could co-operate (Whiting, 1954). Chen Duxiu, who had always mistrusted Sun Yat-sen, was reluctant to go along with this policy (Schwartz, 1979; Feigon, 1983), but the Comintern representative in China, Maring, was able to impose Moscow's authority on the fledgling CCP and by 1922, at the second party congress, it was noted that the most urgent task of the proletariat was to unite with 'democratic groups' against feudal militarism and imperialism (Schwartz, 1979, p. 39). The party made it clear, however, that within such a democratic alliance the workers had to continue to fight for their own interests.

Sun Yat-sen, meanwhile, was seeking to expand his base in the south. Since 1917 he had been dependent on local warlords and twice had been ejected from Guangzhou. His continued quest for funds brought him into conflict with Britain when he attempted to appropriate the Guangzhou customs revenue for his own southern-based government (Wilbur, 1976), and his increasingly vociferous condemnation of foreign imperialism in China marked him as a dangerous radical in the eyes of the western powers. Sun began to look to the Soviet Union as a possible source of aid. He had met Maring as early as 1920 and spoken highly of Lenin's New Economic Policy, which he compared to his own Principle of People's Livelihood. Sun was also attracted to Bolshevik party organization, whose discipline and *esprit de corps* he wanted the Guomindang to emulate.

In January 1923 Sun met with another Comintern representative, Adolph Joffe, and they issued a joint manifesto calling for co-operation between the Guomindang and CCP. Sun agreed to allow the CCP to retain its separate existence but insisted that CCP members enter the Guomindang as individuals rather than as a party. The first United Front was formalized later that year, despite opposition from the right wing of the Guomindang which viewed the CCP with suspicion. Leading communists, such as Li Dazhao, were enthusiastic about the new policy and Mao Zedong was to throw himself wholeheartedly into United-Front work, a fact that was later glossed over by the communist authorities after 1949. Yet it was natural that Li Dazhao and Mao Zedong, both ardent nationalists, should be attracted to the anti-imperialist programme of the United Front. For Mao, the desire to see a revived, strong and *respected* China was a crucial aspect of his early political thought (Schram, 1966; Womack, 1982).

With the United Front, Sun Yat-sen now had access to Soviet military and financial aid. He assumed, unlike the right wing of the Guomindang, that the CCP would not present a threat and that it would ultimately be absorbed into the much larger Guomindang. The CCP, for its part, hoped to use the United Front to expand its membership and gain control of the mass organizations that began to be created under Guomindang auspices. For the Soviet Union, the United Front served its own national interests, since it could now hope to have an increasing influence over a potentially powerful force that would oppose the western powers in China; at the same time Moscow argued that the CCP could eventually take over leadership of the revolution from within and hence fulfil long-term revolutionary aims.

The Soviet Union's tendency, however, to subordinate the interests of the Chinese revolution to its own national interests (illustrated by that fact that foreign policy was made by both the People's Commissariat for Foreign Affairs, whose priority was to enhance the interests of the Soviet state, and the Moscow-dominated Comintern, which promoted international revolution) was clearly seen in the attempt by Moscow to reach agreement with the Beijing-based warlord government at the same time as it was sponsoring the anti-warlord and anti-imperialist United Front in the south. This culminated in a 1924 treaty, which established diplomatic relations between Beijing and Moscow and which provided for joint management of the Chinese Eastern Railway, a Russian railway concession in Manchuria that was originally to have been returned to China in accordance with the Soviet government's desire in 1919 to return all concessions acquired by Tsarist Russia in the nineteenth century (Whiting, 1954; Mancall, 1984).

With the help of Russian advisers and financial assistance Sun proceeded to re-organize the Guomindang into a highly disciplined organization. In particular he relied on Mikhail Borodin, the most important and energetic of the Russian advisers, who was to remain in China until the break-up of the United Front in 1927 (Jacobs, 1981). Borodin convinced Sun that the party would have to mobilize workers and peasants in the revolution to defeat warlordism and imperialism. Party bureaux dealing with propaganda, organization, labour, peasants and women were soon created. At the same time a military academy was established at Whampoa, near Guangzhou, to train officers for a new and ideologically motivated army. Like the Russian Red Army, this new revolutionary army was to have political commissars attached to all units to ensure correct ideological training. The commandant of the Whampoa Academy was Chiang Kai-shek (1887–1975), who had received military training in Japan before 1911 and had become closely associated with Sun Yat-sen. Chiang's association with Sun was also cemented by personal ties since his wife was the sister of Sun Yat-sen's wife, Soong Qingling. The Soongs were a wealthy family which was to exert considerable influence on Chinese politics during the ensuing decades; another sister was to marry H. Kung, a future finance minister in the nationalist government, while a brother, T.V. Soong, was also to serve as finance minister and head numerous business and economic organizations after 1928 (Seagrave, 1985). Although not advertized at the time, Chiang also had close links with the Shanghai underworld, an asset that was to pay dividends in 1927 and 1928 (see next section).

The CCP quickly acquired influence and positions within the re-organized Guomindang. At the first National Congress of the Guomindang in January 1924 communists (including Li Dazhao and Mao Zedong) were elected to the Central Executive Committee. Communists, such as Zhou Enlai (1898–1976), were political commissars at the Whampoa Academy. Communists also headed the Peasant and Organization Bureaux and held top positions in the Labour Bureau (Schram, 1966; Wilbur, 1983). In fact, it was through its United Front with the Guomindang that the CCP began to pay more attention to the peasantry (Hofheinz, 1977). Although Peng Pai, the son of a landlord who had joined the CCP in 1921, had begun to organize tenant farmers near Guangzhou and helped to create a Peasants Union in 1922 (Marks, 1984, pp. 152–281; Galbiati, 1985), the CCP leadership was initially sceptical of the possibility of expanding into rural areas. It was not until after 1923 that the party created its own peasant committee. Peng Pai went on to become a leading member of the Peasant Bureau and was the first director of the Peasant Movement Training Institute set up by the

Guomindang in 1924 to train rural cadres. Peasant associations campaigning for rent reductions began to be formed throughout Guangdong province, and played a role in the Guomindang's struggle with local warlords. It was while serving as director of the Peasant Movement Training Institute in 1926 that Mao Zedong himself came to appreciate the enormous revolutionary potential of the peasantry.

With the death of Sun Yat-sen in 1925 power within the Guomindang began to gravitate towards Chiang Kai-shek who as commander of the National Revolutionary Army and chairman of the Military Council, exerted increasing influence over the civilian wing of the party, which was under the leadership of Wang Jingwei (1883–1941). Wang had been a close colleague of Sun's since their time spent together fomenting anti-Manchu revolution before 1911 and was associated with the left wing of the party. Since both Wang and Chiang claimed the mantle of succession to Sun Yat-sen, a conflict between them developed, which was to lead to a split within the party during 1926–7.

The Guomindang and CCP, meanwhile, reaped the benefits of a growing anti-imperialist tide in China after 1923 and membership of both parties expanded rapidly. The CCP membership for example grew from 130 in 1922 to 60,000 in 1927 (Wilbur, 1983). Anti-imperialist feelings reached a fever pitch with the 30 May Incident in 1925. Ten days earlier Chinese workers protesting against the closure of a Japanese textile mill in Shanghai had been fired upon by Japanese guards and one worker had been killed. On 30 May 1925 students and workers held demonstrations to condemn the Japanese action in particular and protest against foreign privilege in general. The British commander of the International Settlement police force in Shanghai ordered his men to fire on the crowd and twelve people were killed. The incident aroused a storm of protest not only in Shanghai but in all other major cities (Isaacs, 1961, pp. 70–3; Clifford, 1979). Strikes and boycotts in Shanghai and Guangzhou brought economic activity to a virtual standstill, and British and Japanese consulates were attacked.

It was at this point that the Guangzhou regime declared itself the National Government and plans were made for the military unification of China. Chiang's National Revolutionary Army had already proved its worth in local campaigns against the Guangdong warlord, Chen Jiongming. Militarists from the neighbouring province of Guangxi decided to join forces with the Guomindang and their armies were renamed as units of the National Revolutionary Army. These militarists (Bai Chongxi and Li Zongren), known as the Guangxi clique, had been active in promoting reform in their own province and hoped to use their co-operation with the Guomindang as a springboard for national influence (Lary, 1974). A precedent had been set whereby former warlords and their armies were co-opted by the revolutionary forces.

Initially, both Chen Duxiu and Moscow were lukewarm towards the idea of a Northern Expedition. Chen, in particular, feared that such a campaign would merely enhance Chiang Kai-shek's military power. Chiang, however, demonstrated his growing power within the Guomindang by carrying out what became known as the 'March Coup' of 1926. In that month he ordered that Russian advisers be placed under house arrest and declared that members of the CCP would henceforth not be permitted to head party bureaux. CCP membership on party committees was also reduced (Isaacs, 1961; Harrison, 1972; Guillermaz, 1972). At the same time Wang Jingwei was forced into retirement.

Although Chiang now seemed to be publicly backing the Guomindang right wing, which had consistently demanded the expulsion of communists from the party, he adopted a more conciliatory tone after the 'coup', since he still needed the support of the CCP and Moscow in the coming campaign against the warlords. Stalin, for his part, was anxious that the United Front should continue. Within Russia, Stalin's ideological and political differences with Trotsky (which were to lead to Trotsky's eventual expulsion from the Bolshevik party and exile from Russia) had repercussions on the perceptions he had of the situation in China. Thus, while Trotsky opposed the CCP's co-operation with the bourgeoisie (i.e. the Guomindang) and called for the immediate establishment of Soviets, Stalin insisted that the Guomindang represented a four-class bloc (large bourgeoisie, petty bourgeoisie, workers and peasants) and that therefore the CCP needed to remain in the United Front to guarantee its continuing influence over the masses. As will be noted later, Stalin's insistence that the CCP uphold the United-Front policy – to have recommended withdrawal would have validated Trotsky's stance on China and hence would have weakened Stalin's attempt to assert his own ideological leadership – was very nearly to result in the CCP's total annihilation (North, 1953; Brandt, 1958; Isaacs, 1962; Schwartz, 1979).

The United Front therefore held. Chiang released the Russian advisers and, with the support of the CCP and Moscow, the Northern Expedition got underway in the summer of 1926. Against the numerically superior but poorly co-ordinated warlord armies, the National Revolutionary Army was able to enlist considerable mass support (Wilbur, 1968,1983; Jordan, 1976). Very often militant action by peasants and workers preceded the nationalist advance. There were widespread strikes in all major industrial centres, while in the provinces of Hunan and Hubei there was an enormous increase in the number of peasant associations, with a reported membership of over 2 million by the beginning of 1927 (Isaacs, 1961, p. 113).

These associations went beyond the usual call for rent reductions and encouraged direct appropriation of the land, frequently attacking landlords in the process.

Mao Zedong visited Hunan in 1926 and witnessed at first hand the revolution that was occurring in the countryside. He wrote a report on his findings, which has since become one of the classic texts of Chinese communisim. In his 'Report of an Investigation into the Peasant Movement in Hunan', Mao drew the party's attention to the spontaneous struggle by peasants against 'corrupt officials, local bullies and evil gentry'. In contrast to the orthodox Marxist view, which portrayed peasants as essentially conservatives exhibiting a 'petty bourgeois mentality', who would have to be led by a more revolutionary urban proletariat, Mao enthusiastically claimed that the real revolution was already taking place in the countryside and implied that the party risked losing leadership of the revolution if it did not move quickly to involve itself in the peasants' struggle:

> In a very short time, several hundred million peasants in China's central, southern, and northern provinces will rise like a tornado or tempest – a force so extraordinarily swift and violent that no power, however great, will be able to suppress it. They will break through all the trammels that now bind them and push forward along the road to liberation. They will send all imperialists, warlords, corrupt officials, local bullies and evil gentry to their graves. All revolutionary parties and all revolutionary comrades will stand before them to be tested, to be accepted or rejected by them. To march at their head and lead them? To follow in the rear, gesticulating at them and criticizing them? To face them as opponents? Every Chinese is free to choose among the three, but circumstances demand that a quick decision be made. (Quoted in Schram, 1963, pp. 179–80)

Although, as was noted earlier, Peng Pai had begun to organize peasant unions in the early 1920s, among the CCP leadership as a whole it was still assumed that the revolution would primarily be based in the cities. For the first time, a prominent member of the CCP was claiming that the peasantry was the leading force of the revolution. Mao's report was also clear testimony to his populist faith, evident since May Fourth days, in the revolutionary potential of the masses (Womack, 1982). His implied criticism that the party had lost touch with real events going on in the countryside was a reflection of his disdain for 'bookish intellectuals' that was to remain with him throughout his life. (Mao himself had attended both middle school and normal school.)

Mao's confidence that a mobilized peasantry would sweep all

31

before it (with no reference to the guidance and leadership to be provided by the party and urban proletariat) is an example of what some historians have called Mao's 'voluntaristic' belief in the ability of conscious human activity to overcome all objective barriers. As Meisner (1977, p. 41) notes, this implied 'that revolution in China need not be dependent upon any predetermined levels of social and economic development, and that revolutionary action need not be restrained by inherited orthodox Marxist–Leninist formulas'. As such Mao's report was the first significant step in the process whereby he would adapt Marxism–Leninism to Chinese conditions, a process which was later to be defined as the 'Sinification' of Marxism.

By the end of 1926 the nationalist forces had taken control of the provinces of Hunan, Hubei, Jiangxi and Fujian. In addition to co-opting local warlords along the way, the nationalists also obtained the support of more important militarists like Yan Xishan and Feng Yuxiang, who, like the Guangxi Clique, were to gain top positions in the Guomindang hierarchy while still retaining essential control of their own armies.

The increasingly militant mass movement, however, sharpened the differences between the left and right wings of the Guomindang, with the former arguing that it was a positive development and the latter demanding that it be restrained. The foreign powers, too, viewed events with increasing alarm. As nationalist forces reached the Yangzi, the British concession areas in Hankou and Jiujiang were overrun, while in early 1927 the British, American and Japanese consulates in Nanjing were attacked, which prompted quick reprisals in the form of joint British and American naval bombardment of the city.

As Wang Jingwei, Soong Qingling and others associated with the Guomindang left wing began to set up a government in Wuhan, Chiang Kai-shek proceeded to Shanghai. A series of strikes during the previous months had paralysed the city and played an important part in preventing the local warlord, Sun Chuanfang, from mounting effective resistance against the advancing nationalist forces. In April 1927, less than one month after being welcomed by the workers, Chiang turned on his erstwhile leftist allies and brutally suppressed all trade unions in the city, arresting and executing all those accused of being in league with the communists. Chiang's actions were supported and abetted by both the Shanghai business and merchant classes, who feared the disruptive effects of militant labour activity, and the foreign powers, who favoured a quick return to normality. Chiang was also able to enlist the help of Shanghai's underworld, particularly the Green Gang, a secret society involved in drug trafficking and operating gambling houses and brothels, in rounding up and shooting communists and their supporters (Isaacs, 1961).

This 'white terror' was extended to other cities under Chiang's control.

The nationalist government at Wuhan condemned Chiang's action (prompting Chiang to set up his own government in Nanjing) but its position became increasingly untenable. Although it had the support of a number of militarists jealous of Chiang's power, these generals were opposed to the continuing appropriation of land by peasant associations in the Hunan/Hubei countryside since many of them owned land themselves or were related to landowners. Labour strikes in the city of Wuhan itself also placed the government in an awkward position as it attempted to steer a middle course between satisfying union demands and restraining the 'excesses' of the mass movement. The CCP, meanwhile, was the victim of contradictory advice from Moscow. On the one hand Stalin instructed the CCP to co-operate with the Wuhan regime, on the basis that it represented the genuinely revolutionary wing of the Guomindang (now defined by Stalin as representing a 'three class bloc', since Chiang Kai-shek, as the spokesman of the large bourgeoisie, had now shown his true reactionary colours) and on the other, advised the party to arm the peasants, eliminate unreliable generals from the army, and strive to replace 'reactionary elements' within the Wuhan government itself.

Not surprisingly, Wuhan government leaders became increasingly suspicious of their CCP allies. Faced with sabotage from within and mutiny from its military supporters, who now began to take matters into their own hands and embarked on a ruthless campaign to suppress the peasant movement, the Wuhan regime dissolved itself, and the two wings of the Guomindang were formally united once more, with Chiang's own power and prestige greatly enhanced. Chiang then continued with the Northern Expedition and in 1928, with the help of Yan Xishan and Feng Yuxiang, succeeded in taking Beijing and forcing Zhang Zuolin to flee northwards to his home base in Manchuria. A new national government was formally proclaimed, with its capital to be situated in Nanjing.

The United Front had ended in total disaster for the CCP, with its membership decimated and urban base smashed. Chen Duxiu was made the scapegoat and accused of 'right-wing opportunism' (i.e. failure to encourage the mass movement). In August 1927 he was replaced as secretary-general of the party by Qu Qiubai. The party thereupon launched a series of insurrections, hoping to make use of mutinies within Guomindang army ranks and seize key towns and cities.

One of them, known as the Autumn Harvest Uprising, designed to capture Changsha (Hunan) in September 1927, was led by Mao. His insistence that a more organized military force be created under an independent CCP banner (rather than under the banner of the 'revolutionary left Guomindang' as laid down by the party leaders) and that a larger base area be formed instead of merely attacking a few cities brought him a rebuke from the CCP Central Committee (now underground in Shanghai), which would come to view Mao as a reckless military adventurer (Schram, 1966). The Autumn Harvest Uprising failed and Mao took the remnants of his force, comprising landless peasants, vagrants and brigands, to Jingganshan, on the Hunan–Jiangxi border. There he was to meet up with Zhu De, one of the leaders of an earlier insurrection, and they began to build up a new military force which was to be the foundation of the Red Army. The CCP's woes were completed in December 1927 when its last attempt at urban insurrection, the Guangzhou Commune, was bloodily suppressed. Henceforth the Chinese revolution would be based in the countryside.

The Nanjing Decade, 1928–37

When the Guomindang declared itself the national government in 1928 it was acting in accordance with Sun Yat-sen's principle of political tutelage. By this Sun had meant that the party would have to guide the political destiny of the nation until such time as the people were prepared for democracy, after which a constitution would be promulgated. Yet, although institutions of government were created in Nanjing, the Guomindang regime was never able to exert total control of the country beyond the immediate surrounding provinces. Large areas of China, such as the province of Sichuan, were still ruled by pre-1928 militarists, who recognized the Nanjing government but successfully blocked its attempts to reduce their power (Kapp, 1973). Those militarists who had joined the Guomindang during the Northern Expedition, like Yan Xishan and Feng Yuxiang, were appointed members of the Guomindang Central Executive Committee but persistently refused to disband or reduce their armies. Furthermore, the government was beset throughout the 1930s with increasing Japanese encroachment in the north (see next chapter), a growing communist threat in the south, and a series of revolts by disgruntled militarists.

Chiang Kai-shek was to use his military campaigns against the communists to extend Nanjing's political control during the 1930s so that, according to one historian, the government ruled 25 per cent of the country (comprising 66 per cent of the population) in 1937, in contrast to the 8 per cent of the country (comprising 20 per cent of the population) it had controlled in 1929 (Eastman, 1974, p. 281). However, a measure of the regime's weak hold on the country can be seen in the fact that Nanjing derived virtually all of its revenues from the modern sector concentrated in Shanghai. Furthermore, the government's expenditures in 1933, for example, represented a mere 2.4 per cent of China's total domestic product (Coble, 1980, p. 9).

Despite the extravagant claims of one political scientist that the Guomindang regime laid the groundwork for the creation of a nation state (Bedeski, 1981), the regime itself was riddled with factionalism and corruption and showed scant commitment to genuine social or economic reform (Eastman, 1974). Those measures which were passed, such as the land rent reduction law in 1930, were never effectively implemented, principally because of the regime's unwillingness to counter the influence of local rural elites (Bianco, 1971). Rural areas under Nanjing's control also suffered an increased tax burden as peasants were subjected to increased surcharges on the land tax imposed by local district governments (Eastman, 1974). Since most of Nanjing's expenditures were used for military purposes little was done to promote economic development. The construction of roads and railways, for example, was carried out for strategic aims rather than for developing the economy. Social reform consisted primarily of Chiang's New Life Movement, launched in 1934, to encourage frugality, simplicity and hygiene among the people as well as impressing upon them the wisdom of Confucian morality, an indication of the essentially conservative nature of the regime.

The Guomindang also took little heed of the interests of the urban business and merchant classes. Although earlier studies have portrayed the Guomindang as either the hireling of the newly emerging urban bourgeoisie or as the representative of rural and urban elites (Isaacs, 1961; Moore, 1966), recent research has shown that the Guomindang had no intention of allowing the urban capitalists to acquire political influence, while at the same time it resorted to extortion, increased taxes and forced purchase of government bonds in order to milk the modern sector of the economy (Coble, 1980; Bergère, 1983). By 1936 the government had taken control of the most important private banks, which were compelled to subscribe to government bonds. In this way, as Coble (1980) remarks, the urban capitalists became dependent on the Nanjing regime. Speculation in government bonds was rife, particularly among government ministers themselves (including H. Kung, a minister of finance and Chiang's brother-in-law), some of whom served as bank directors.

Chiang's constant need for revenue to fuel his military campaigns against either the communists or recalcitrant militarists made him oblivious to the needs of native industry. Thus, even after tariff autonomy was achieved in 1929, one of the few concrete achievements during the decade, rates on imports were not raised unduly (which might have enhanced the competition of native industry) for fear that this might lead to a decline in imports and hence less customs revenue for the government (Coble, 1980).

The Guomindang regime was therefore not the spokesman of the urban capitalists. Yet neither did it plan to eliminate private enterprise altogether in favour of a planned socialist economy, as the anticapitalist bias of Guomindang propaganda might have suggested (capitalists were accused of being only concerned with their individual interests at the expense of those of the nation). As a recent study shows, despite the desire of some Guomindang members to unite with the more radical and politically active elements of the merchant community – which tended to be representative of small-scale business and industry – against the merchant elite that had traditionally dominated the modern banking and industrial sectors, Chiang called a halt to further mass campaigns after 1928, arguing that they would be detrimental to social unity. The merchant elite was not displaced but was merely co-opted by the regime (Fewsmith, 1984).

The Guomindang itself was split into various cliques or factions, whose bitter rivalry Chiang was able skilfully to manipulate in order to ensure his own pre-eminence, a position that was given formal recognition in 1938 when Chiang was awarded the title of 'leader' (*zongcai*). Yet it is a curious fact that although Chiang was able to impose strict press censorship and effectively hinder any attempt by liberal intellectuals to create new political organizations or pressure groups – for example, those demanding the promulgation of a permanent constitution which would establish full democracy, something the regime was never to achieve – he was unable to eliminate corruption or inefficiency within the party or government itself. This was despite the fact that in 1932 Chiang sponsored the creation of an elite corps within the Guomindang to enhance his own personal leadership and stamp out corruption amongst party and government bureaucrats. Known as the Blue Shirts, the corps drew inspiration from European fascism (Eastman, 1974; Chang, 1986). Yet even this organization made little impact and was disbanded in 1938, although Chiang's admiration for Nazi Germany resulted in the employment of high-ranking German officers during the 1930s to train selected regiments of his army (Kirby, 1984).

Chiang was able to utilize the expertise of these German officers in his military campaigns against the communists. By 1929 Mao, already relieved of his position on the party's central committee for the failure of the Autumn Harvest Uprising, had moved to southern Jiangxi, where he began to establish a base area. During these years Mao was virtually acting independently of the party leadership in Shanghai, which branded him a military adventurer for his strategy of guerilla warfare and enlistment of the rural *lumpenproletariat* (labourers, landless peasants, bandits and secret society members) in his fledgling Red Army (Rue, 1966).

Nevertheless, the CCP Central Committee, now under the leadership of Li Lisan, called on Mao's force to participate in a new campaign of co-ordinated rural and urban uprisings in accordance with Stalin's confident assertion that a new revolutionary 'high tide' existed throughout the world due to the Great Depression (and also to take advantage of renewed fighting between Chiang and mutinous generals). In 1930 attempts to take and occupy the cities of Changsha, Nanchang and Wuhan failed, principally due to the lack of mass support, and Mao withdrew once more to his base area in Jiangxi, convinced more than ever that the consolidation of a self-sufficient territorial base had to be given priority.

Li Lisan was recalled to Moscow in disgrace, where he was severely reprimanded for his 'adventurism' and 'petty bourgeois chauvinism', the last charge being made because Li had proclaimed China as imperialism's weakest link and hence had attributed to the Chinese revolution world-wide significance (Thornton, 1969). Party leadership now fell into the hands of a group known as the Twenty-Eight Bolsheviks, because they had all studied in Moscow between 1926 and 1930. Led by Wang Ming, Bo Gu and Lo Fu, they were loyal supporters of the Comintern line and were even more critical of Mao than the previous leadership had been. In November 1931 Mao invited party leaders to attend the first All-China Congress of Soviets in Ruijin, which formally proclaimed the establishment of the Jiangxi Soviet Republic and elected Mao as chairman of the Soviet government (Waller, 1973). The Jiangxi Soviet was, in fact, one of a number of rural soviets created at this time in central and southern China, but the Jiangxi Soviet was the largest, comprising thirty-six districts with a population of up to 3 million (Harrison, 1971, p. 199).

When the party leadership in Shanghai moved permanently to Ruijin in 1932–3 Mao's influence was gradually reduced. Although he retained his post as chairman of the soviet government it became largely an honorary one. Real power lay with the Politburo, the party's highest policy-making organ, which was dominated by the Twenty-Eight Bolsheviks. They were particularly critical of Mao's land distribution policy and his guerilla tactics. In contrast to his more radical land policy while at Jingganshan in 1929, when land belonging to both landlords and rich peasants (i.e. land-owning peasants who worked the land themselves as well as renting a part of it to others) was confiscated and redistributed to poor peasants, Mao's land reform law in 1931 allowed rich peasants to receive an allotment of land provided they tilled it themselves. This was considered by the party leadership as evidence of Mao's failure to adopt a strong class line and after 1933 a harsher attitude was taken towards rich peasants. Yet Mao's land distribution policy was in accord with his strategy of mobilizing as much rural support as possible, while at the same time his encouragement of poor peasant associations to participate actively in the confiscation and redistribution of land belonging to landlords reflected his belief that land reform was to have a political, as well as an economic, significance. The involvement of peasant associations in such a process was an aspect of what Mao would call the 'mass line' (Kim, 1973).

After 1933 Mao's emphasis on flexible, guerilla warfare against invading nationalist forces was replaced by a stress on a more orthodox strategy of positional warfare. Between 1930 and 1934 Chiang Kai-shek launched five campaigns of 'encirclement and extermination' against the Jiangxi Soviet. The first four had failed, but the fifth, begun in October 1933, was more successful. On the advice of General Hans von Seeckt, head of the German military mission, Chiang adopted a policy of economic strangulation, blockading the soviet with an array of fortresses and pillboxes. The Red Army suffered a series of disastrous defeats and in October 1934 it was decided to evacuate the Jiangxi Soviet and establish a new base area in the north-west. Thus began the Long March, an epic journey of 6,000 miles which took the beleaguered communist forces to the province of Shaanxi. Approximately 100,000 set off from Jiangxi but only 8,000 reached Shaanxi one year later.

During the course of the Long March Mao demanded the convening of an enlarged Politburo conference at Zunyi (Guizhou province) in January 1935, which criticized the errors of the party leadership during the last years of the Jiangxi Soviet. More importantly, the Zunyi conference marked the beginning of Mao's eventual leadership of the party. Mao was not only elected to the Politburo and appointed head of the general secretariat but was also awarded the important post of director of the Military Affairs committee (Harrison, 1972; Guillermaz, 1972; Thornton, 1973).

By 1936 the CCP had established new headquarters at Yanan in north Shaanxi which, owing to its inhospitable terrain, was relatively safe from possible attack. It was here that Mao over the next few years was to consolidate his political and ideological leadership of the party. Meanwhile, there occurred a temporary respite in Chiang's campaign against the communists as both sides agreed to co-operate against a common enemy – Japan.

3 The War of Resistance Against Japan

The war that broke out between China and Japan in 1937 was the final act of a drama in which Japan had sought to preserve her economic and political rights in China in the face of both a reinvigorated Chinese nationalism and the increasing hostility of Britain and the United States (Jansen, 1972). At the same time Japan saw the war as the first step in the creation of a new order in East Asia, one in which China would finally realize that her true interests lay in partnership with Japan against the twin evils of Soviet communism and Anglo-Saxon liberal democracy (Storry 1979). Japan's actions in China, however, revealed the very fragile distinction between 'partnership' and domination, while at the same time Japanese government leaders failed to understand that the idea of a new order in East Asia never appealed to the Chinese because Chinese nationalism since the turn of the century had been directed just as much against Japan as against the West.

Contrary to initial assumptions on Japan's part that the 'China Incident' (as it was called) would be over in a few months, the war was to last eight years and represented an enormous drain of Japan's human and material resources. By 1941 Japan was also at war with the United States and Britain and events were set in motion that would lead ultimately to Japan's total military defeat, the end of the European empires in South-East Asia and the emergence of the United States as the greatest power in the Pacific region, and the creation of a new communist China.

The Origins of Japanese Imperialism

Since the Meiji Restoration in 1868, when the feudal rule of the Tokugawa had been replaced by a centralized government under the Meiji emperor, Japanese government policy had aimed to create a wealthy and strong nation in order to meet the threat of an expanding West. This quest for security was also an important motive in early Japanese expansionism, although such a policy could also rely on

39

the support of radical nationalists outside the government bent on extending Japanese influence in Asia, particularly China. By the end of the nineteenth century it was also assumed that Japan needed to become an imperialist power in order both to emulate and to compete with the West (Jansen, 1984). Such an assumption, in addition to increasing contempt for China's failure to modernize, dispelled earlier hopes among some Japanese that Japan could repay her cultural debt to China, dating from the eighth century, by joining with her in common cause against the West.

In 1895 Japan formally entered the ranks of the imperialist powers in Asia after defeating China in a war fought over who would have the dominant influence in Korea. By the Treaty of Shimonoseki, not only was Japan's predominance in Korea recognized but she also gained all the rights and privileges enjoyed by the West in China and acquired the island of Taiwan (formerly part of the province of Fujian). In 1900, for the first time, Japan joined the western powers in military action in China when she participated in the allied expedition to Beijing to relieve the foreign legations besieged by the Boxers. Japan's status was further enhanced in 1902 when Tokyo signed an alliance with Britain, the principal aim of which was to check Russian influence in Asia.

Russia's growing presence in Manchuria and attempts to extend her influence in north Korea were regarded by Tokyo as a threat to Japan's security. Conflict between the two countries broke out in 1904 and by 1905 Russia sued for peace. For the first time in modern history an Asian country had defeated a western power, a fact not overlooked by reformers and revolutionaries throughout Asia struggling against their European colonial masters. More importantly as far as Japan was concerned, the Treaty of Portsmouth (brought about by the United States' mediation) which ended the war, awarded the leased territory of Port Arthur and the South Manchuria railway to Japan. Over the next thirty years the Japanese presence in Manchuria was to grow and her rights and privileges there came to be regarded as sacred, bought with Japanese blood. A Japanese military force, known as the Kwantung Army, was stationed in the Liaodong peninsula, while the Japanese-controlled South Manchuria Railway Company gradually acquired mining concessions and the right to station railway guards along the line.

As an imperialist power in China on a par with western powers, it seemed that Japan had now attained equality with the West, and yet the relationship between the two remained uneasy. The United States, in particular, began to voice increasing concern after 1905 over the potential threat Japan posed to her security interests in the Pacific, while the blatantly racist nature of anti-Japanese immigration policy in Hawaii (recently annexed by the United States) and California soured relations between the two countries (Iriye, 1967,

1972). Furthermore, the United States' espousal of the open door doctrine (first enunciated in 1899), which called for equality of commerical opportunity among the powers in China irrespective of spheres of influence, clashed with Japan's determination to preserve her economic dominance in Manchuria.

Japan's relationship with China was also ambiguous. On the one hand there were private Japanese individuals who sincerely desired to work and co-operate with Chinese revolutionaries such as Sun Yat-sen in the creation of a modern and democratic China (Jansen, 1954); on the other, the Japanese government, despite frequent pious statements that Japan desired to repay her cultural debt to China by helping her to modernize, treated China with the same arrogance and contempt shown by the other powers and continually sought to expand her privileges there, particularly in Manchuria. Ironically, it was the thousands of admiring Chinese students who flocked to Japan in the early years of the twentieth century who were the first to become painfully aware of the inferior status assigned to the Chinese by many Japanese. Ominously for the future, there were elements among the Japanese army, particularly the Kwantung Army, who began to argue that Japan should go her own way in China and disregard potential criticism or opposition from the western powers.

British and American suspicion of Japan intensified both in the wake of the 1911 revolution, when the Kwantung Army attempted to foster an autonomy movement in Manchuria, and during the First World War, when Japan seized the opportunity to acquire the German concession in Shandong and impose the Twenty-One Demands on Yuan Shikai's government (see chapter 1).

The Washington System and its Breakdown

In 1921–2 the United States organized the Washington Conference, which affirmed the powers' respect for the sovereignty and territorial integrity of China. The principle of equal economic opportunity in China was also upheld and the notion of 'spheres of influence' was condemned. Much to the satisfaction of the United States, the Anglo-Japanese alliance was allowed to lapse, to be replaced by a four-power treaty (United States, Britain, Japan and France) which provided for mutual consultation if any threats arose with regard to their rights in China. As further indication of potential harmony and co-operation among the powers, a naval treaty limited construction of capital ships (with Japan accepting a lower ratio *vis-à-vis* Britain and the United States) and halted any further build-up of fortifications in the western Pacific. Finally, Japan agreed at the Washington Conference to return Qingdao and the Shandong railway to China (Thorne, 1972, pp. 27–8).

41

Iriye (1965) believes that the period 1922–5 represented a lost opportunity for the powers to implement the aims of the Washington Conference and create a new framework of international relations in East Asia. He argues that, owing to chronic instability within China and the bewildering succession of warlord regimes, the emergence of a new factor in Chinese politics in the shape of the Guomindang–CCP United Front supported by a country not party to the Washington Conference, the Soviet Union, and continuing suspicion among the powers themselves, it was inevitable that each power would eventually decide to act unilaterally in China to safeguard its rights.

Nevertheless, it should not be forgotten that despite the Washington Conference's rhetorical support for China's independence and territorial integrity, the powers did not at this time envisage an end to the unequal treaty system (China had not even been invited to the Washington Conference). The one concession which was made was the proposal to hold a tariff conference in 1925–6 to negotiate the gradual return of tariff autonomy to China. Disagreements arose at the conference, however, and each power decided to make its own arrangements with the Chinese government (Borg, 1947; Iriye, 1965; Louis, 1971). Although tariff autonomy for China was formally recognized in 1929, it was not to be until 1943 that Britain and the United States, as a sop to Chiang Kai-shek, whose role in the war against Japan was considered vital, would agree to end their privilege of extra-territoriality in China (a privilege that had become largely irrelevant anyway because of the Japanese occupation).

What none of the powers had anticipated, however, was the rapid growth of anti-imperialism during the 1920s and the increasing importance of the United Front. While Britain and the United States wavered between armed intervention to punish the excesses of the Northern Expedition and an attitude of 'wait and see', Japan, perceiving the growing split between the left and right wing of the Guomindang, sought to negotiate with Chiang Kai-shek. At the same time Tokyo was determined, as she had always been, that her economic interests in China would not be threatened by continuing war and unrest. Thus twice, in 1927 and 1928, prime minister Tanaka Giichi despatched troops to Shandong to protect Japanese lives and property there, which resulted in armed clashes with Chiang Kai-shek's advancing nationalist forces (Nobuya, 1972; Morton, 1980). A new wave of anti-Japanese sentiment led to boycotts of Japanese goods, ironically at the very time that Britain and the United States were adopting a more conciliatory attitude towards Chiang Kai-shek, whose promise to put an end to all anti-foreign excesses and crack down on labour unions and communists gave him credibility as an upholder of 'law and order'.

Japan's economic stake in China, particularly in Manchuria, was far greater than that of either Britain or the United States. Whereas by 1931, for example, China represented 81.9 per cent of Japan's total foreign investment, two-thirds of which was in Manchuria, China represented only 6 per cent of Britain's total overseas investments and less that 1.5 per cent for the United States (Thorne, 1972, pp. 32–3). Japan also supplied one quarter (in value) of China's imports and took a similar proportion of her exports, again the largest share coming from Manchuria. Manchuria, in fact, had become a vital source of minerals essential for Japan's programme of industrial and military development. It was also increasingly perceived as a suitable region for Japan's surplus population. By 1930 military planners in the Kwantung Army, such as Ishiwara Kanji, were arguing that Manchuria would be crucial for any future war effort against either the Soviet Union or the United States (Peattie, 1975).

Lower-ranking officers in the Kwantung Army engineered an incident near Mukden in 1931 (a section of the South Manchuria railway was blown up), which was used as a pretext to launch a military offensive in Manchuria (Ogata, 1964). Despite calls from Tokyo for restraint, the Kwantung Army extended its sphere of operations and Manchuria was overrun within five months. In 1932 hostilities between Chinese and Japanese troops also broke out in Shanghai. Chiang Kai-shek, preoccupied with his campaign against the communists, appealed to the League of Nations. Despite a report issued by a League of Nations investigative mission (the Lytton Commission), which pointed to Japan as the aggressor, and the announcement by the United States Secretary of State, Henry Stimson, that Washington would not recognize any settlement brought about by force (known as the non-recognition doctrine), little was done. In 1932 the Kwantung Army created the puppet state of Manchukuo and installed Puyi, the last Qing emperor, as a figurehead ruler. The government in Tokyo was confronted with a *fait accompli* and henceforth was to be subject to increasing pressure from the Kwantung Army, which had supporters within the General Staff in Tokyo, to adopt a stonger line with regard to its China policy. As Crowley (1966) has shown, however, there were divisions within the armed services themselves concerning priorities. The army, anticipating war with the Soviet Union, tended to advocate an expansionist policy in China to secure Japan's flank in Manchuria, while the navy argued that the principal threat to Japan's security was the United States' naval presence in the Pacific.

Mutual mistrust between Britain and the United States, in addition to their reluctance to antagonize Japan, overtly prevented an effective common stance to deal with Japanese aggression in Manchuria (Thorne, 1972). The League resorted to a moral condemnation but the idea of imposing economic sanctions on Japan was shelved. This was enough, however, to alienate Tokyo and Japan withdrew her membership of the League in 1933. Japan's political isolation from the world community was worsened by the effects of the Great Depression. With the appearance of tariff barriers throughout the world during the 1930s, which threatened Japan's foreign trade, a 'siege mentality' increasingly took hold of Japanese leaders. It was in this context that the East Asian mainland assumed an even more vital importance for Japan. Thus when T.V. Soong, Chiang Kai-shek's finance minister, sought to acquire United States economic assistance and credits through a newly formed state organization, the Reconstruction Finance Corporation, Tokyo vigorously protested, perceiving this move as an attempt to reduce Japan's own economic influence in China (Borg, 1964; Coble, 1980).

Meanwhile, from 1933 onwards, the Japanese army in Manchuria attempted to expand its influence in north China. Guomindang political influence in the region was gradually whittled away and in 1935 the Japanese sponsored the creation of an East Hebei Autonomous Council under their influence. With Japanese connivance large-scale silver and narcotics smuggling became widespread (Boyle, 1972). In 1936 the Japanese foreign minister, Hirota Koki, published the governments' demands, the acceptance of which, he insisted, had to form the basis of any understanding reached with Nanjing – recognition of Japan's special position in north China and an end to all anti-Japanese demonstrations in the region, Sino-Japanese collaboration against communism, and the employment of Japanese advisers by the Chinese government. Japan's increasingly aggressive stance was further illustrated when Tokyo signed the anti-Comintern Pact with Nazi Germany in the same year.

The Second United Front

Throughout the early 1930s Chiang Kai-shek argued that defeat of the CCP had to take precedence over everything else, but increasing numbers of people began to criticize what they saw as Chiang's appeasement of Japan. In 1933 a division of Chiang's own army, the Nineteenth Route Army, which was stationed in Fujian to fight the communists and had previously fought the Japanese at Shanghai in 1932, rose up in revolt and proclaimed the creation of a new government. The rebels called for an end to the civil war and for resistance against Japan (Eastman, 1974). Although Chiang succeeded in suppressing the insurrection in 1934, criticism of his policy continued. The CCP itself began calling for a united front of all democratic forces within the country to resist Japan, two years before the Comintern's instruction to communist parties in 1935 to form alliances with anti-fascist groups. In December 1935 there were student demonstrations in Beijing protesting against the government's

44

lack of resolve in dealing with Japanese aggression in north China (Israel and Klein, 1976).

When Chiang flew to Xian in 1936 to reproach his troops for their lacklustre performance against the communists in Shaanxi, he was promptly placed under house arrest by the commander, Zhang Xueliang. Zhang, who had suffered the ignominy of seeing his native Manchuria overrun by the Japanese, demanded that the military campaign against the communists cease and that all Chinese unite to confront the Japanese threat. He even intimated that he would have Chiang executed as a traitor. Ironically it was through CCP intercession that Zhang was persuaded to release Chiang, on condition that he promise to halt his campaign against the communists and form a united front. It was felt that Chiang's symbolic importance as the head of the central government in Nanjing could contribute to a more effective national unity, a feeling that was shared by the United States and Britain, as well as by the Soviet Union (Wu, 1976).

With Chiang's release in December 1936, the second United Front was established. Unlike in 1923, the CCP was now in a much stronger position, possessing its own military force and controlling specific territory. Nevertheless, the CCP accepted Chiang's overall command and promised to relax its radical policy of land confiscation in the interests of national unity. When, in July 1937, Japanese and Chinese troops clashed near Beijing, both sides refused to compromise. Chiang sent reinforcements and proclaimed all-out resistance to Japan.

The Sino-Japanese War, 1937–45

Tokyo was confident that the war would not last long. By 1938 Japanese forces had taken Beijing, Shanghai, Nanjing (where atrocities against the civilian population were committed), Guangzhou and Wuhan. The nationalist government moved west to Chongqing, in Sichuan province, which was to remain Chiang's headquarters throughout the war. Although Japanese forces occupied the coast and the key urban centres in the north and along the lower Yangzi, they found it impossible to conquer the vast hinterland. After 1939 a stalemate virtually ensued, punctuated by occasional clashes and skirmishes. Yet the China war represented a considerable drain on Japanese manpower. Between 1937 and 1941 up to 750,000 troops were engaged in China, approximately one half of the total strength of the army. By the end of 1945 there were to be 1.2 million Japanese troops (out of a total overseas force of 2.3 million) stationed in China (Hsü, 1983a, p. 611).

In the north-west the communist forces were re-organized as the Eighth Route Army, and they conducted a guerilla campaign against the Japanese, often behind enemy lines. The CCP also created border governments in the region, the most important one being the Shaanxi–Gansu–Ningxia Border Region with Yanan as its capital. During the course of the war the communists were able gradually to enlarge the territory under their control throughout north China (Johnson, 1962).

The Second United Front was tenuous from the very beginning. Although there were CCP representatives (including Zhou Enlai) in Chongqing, Chiang's mistrust of the communists remained, while Mao and other CCP leaders made no secret of the fact that they intended to expand communist influence during the war of resistance. Chiang virtually imposed an economic blockade on Yanan, while mutual antagonism often resulted in armed skirmishes between communist and nationalist forces, the most serious one being the New Fourth Army Incident in 1941 when the communist New Fourth Army, comprising remnants that had remained in east China after 1934, was attacked by nationalist troops as it deployed north of the Yangzi. Yanan, however, rather than Chongqing, became for many Chinese the symbol of national resistance to the Japanese, and thousands of students and intellectuals from cities such as Beijing flocked to Yanan. Such a large influx into the region of outsiders, many of whom joined the communist party, was to cause Mao concern about the ideological 'soundness' of the party (see next section).

For the first years of the war China stood virtually alone against Japan. The Soviet Union initially extended credit to the Chinese government for military supplies and sent volunteer pilots to take part in the defence of cities such as Xian, Chongqing and Hankou. In 1938 and 1939 large-scale fighting broke out between Russian and Japanese troops along the border between the Soviet Union and Manchuria, in which the Japanese suffered heavy losses. Yet after 1939 Russia's aid to China diminished as Stalin's attention became increasingly focused on meeting a possible threat from Nazi Germany. In 1941 Stalin signed a non-aggression treaty with Japan, which signalled the end of Soviet involvement in the China war.

Chiang received little or no aid either from Britain (preoccupied with the situation in Europe) or the United States. Although a small group of American volunteer pilots (the 'Flying Tigers') operated from south-west China, it was not until early 1941 that the United States provided significant credit to Chongqing for the purchase of military goods, in accordance with the Lend Lease Act (Schaller, 1979; Mancall, 1984, pp. 303–5).

By 1938 Tokyo had decided it could no longer deal with Chiang Kai-shek and in November of that year prime minister Konoe announced the creation of a new order in East Asia. Since, Konoe argued, China and Japan were racially and culturally akin, it was natural that the two should co-operate, politically and economically, in defeating both communism and western imperialism. Tokyo's attempt to promote an alternative Chinese regime with which it could deal was complicated by the manoeuvres of the Japanese army in China, which had already begun to sponsor various client regimes in Beijing, Nanjing and Shanghai (Boyle, 1972).

Nevertheless, Wang Jingwei responded to Tokyo's overtures and left Chongqing at the end of 1938, initially in the hope of mediating between Chiang and the Japanese but ultimately with the aim of establishing a new Guomindang regime in Nanjing. A recent study of this 'peace movement', as it was called, maintains that Wang was motivated partly by his keen personal rivalry with Chiang Kai-shek, a rivalry that had persisted since Sun Yat-sen's death, and partly by his sincere desire to bring an end to the war (Bunker, 1971). Although Wang inaugurated a new government in 1940 his hopes of bringing about peace and genuine Sino-Japanese co-operation never materialized. Tokyo was unwilling to grant Wang real influence or power, and the regime lacked credibility from the start (in fact, it was recognized only by Japan and the European fascist powers). Denounced by both the CCP and Chiang Kai-shek as a traitor and having to suffer repeated humiliation at the hands of the Japanese, Wang died in 1944 a bitterly disillusioned man, his only achievement being that Tokyo in 1943 had allowed his regime to take over the foreign concessions in Shanghai.

Japan's ever-increasing need for mineral resources, particularly oil, prompted more ambitious plans for a southward expansion in Asia to embrace the rich oil-fields of the Dutch East Indies (Indonesia). By 1940 Japanese troops were in Indo-China. Relations with the United States deteriorated and Washington placed an embargo on the export of petroleum to Japan. Toyko's decision to carry out a pre-emptive strike on the American naval base at Pearl Harbour in December 1941, which was quickly followed by the capture of Hong Kong, Malaya, Singapore, the Dutch East Indies and the Philippines, dramatically changed the nature of the Sino-Japanese war. With the United States and Britain now directly at war with Japan as well as with Hitler's Germany (which had declared war on the United States shortly after Pearl Harbour), China's resistance to the Japanese was seen as a heroic contribution to the world-wide struggle against fascism (Schaller, 1979). United States aid to China henceforth increased and during the years 1942–5 would amount to over 1 billion US dollars (Mancall, 1984, p. 306).

For Japan the defeat of western imperialism in South-East Asia heralded what Tokyo called the Greater East-Asian Co-Prosperity Sphere (Storry, 1979), but as in China the realities of the Japanese occupation often belied the high-sounding rhetoric of co-operation. Nevertheless, the ease with which Japanese forces had overrun the former western colonies had an enormous impact on the development of Asian nationalism. The myth of the white man's invincibility had been irretrievably shattered and the former colonial masters would have to confront vigorous liberation movements when they returned in 1945 to reclaim their 'possessions'. Interestingly, it is precisely this consequence of the Japanese occupation to which some circles in present-day Japan refer in their attempt to emphasize the more positive aspects of Japan's role in the Asian war.

Although Chiang was made supreme commander of the China theatre of war (within the China–Burma–India theatre) and was now assured of substantial United States aid, he remained unwilling to use his troops in large-scale offensives against the Japanese, preferring to keep his forces intact for the future showdown with the CCP that he knew must come. The American general, Joseph Stilwell, who was attached to Chiang's command after 1942, was continually frustrated in his efforts to persuade Chiang to show greater urgency and constantly complained to Washington of the inefficiency and corruption that he saw prevailing in Chongqing (Tuchman, 1970; Schaller, 1979). Stilwell's complaints were reinforced by the negative reports on the Chongqing government by American foreign service officers in China such as J. Service and J. Davies. President Roosevelt, however, continued to place his faith in Chiang. His continued leadership was seen as a crucial element in Roosevelt's plans for the post-war world, in which a united and democratic China would become one of the Big Four (along with the United States, the Soviet Union and Britain).

Although observers on the spot often commented on the corruption of Chiang's regime, recent studies have also underlined the limitations on Chiang's power (Ch'i 1982; Eastman, 1984). The Guomindang's political control had diminished after 1937 when the government had been compelled to abandon its political and economic stronghold in the east, particularly the provinces of Zhejiang and Jiangsu. Furthermore, Chiang's central government troops constituted only approximately one-fifth of all the nationalist forces. The loyalty and commitment of many army commanders to Chiang Kai-shek were never complete. In provinces such as Sichuan (where the Chongqing government was located), Shanxi and Yunnan, military governors frequently obstructed central control. Mutual rivalries and suspicions prompted everyone to play a waiting game, with no one commander (including Chiang) willing to risk losing troops in any large-scale action. Throughout the war, in fact, there continued to be illicit trade between unoccupied and occupied China, a trade tolerated by the local commanders of both sides (Eastman, 1980). Very often it seemed that more hostility was directed against the communists than against the Japanese. Eastman (1984, p. 138), citing Hubei provincial reports of 1942–3, notes that nationalist operations against the Japanese were defensive and reactive while those against the communists were offensive and involved a larger number of troops.

The ineffectiveness of the nationalist forces was highlighted in stark clarity in 1944 when the Japanese launched their one and only major offensive after 1938 (the Ichigo offensive), which led to advances in the south and south-west. Nationalist resistance was swept aside with brutal ease, prompting Stilwell to insist afterwards that he be given overall command of Chinese troops. Inevitably, this was unacceptable to Chiang and he was able to have Stilwell recalled, an interesting example of the leverage Chiang was able to exert on Washington.

It was a measure of the increasing alienation of the peasantry in the areas under nationalist control that the retreating Chinese troops in the wake of the Ichigo offensive were actually attacked by peasants. Increased taxes and 'contributions', such as the military grain levy, had already worsened the economic plight of the peasantry, and this was aggravated by the arbitrary use of military and labour conscription which particularly affected the less well-off. In Henan a famine in 1942–3 as a result of poor harvests and the military grain levy led to the death of several million people (Eastman,1984, pp. 67–8). By 1945 famine was widespread.

Although the Ichigo offensive enabled Japanese troops to advance to Yunnan and Guizhou in the south-west, the China war by 1944 had, in a sense, assumed a secondary importance in the overall American strategy against Japan. Initially, it had been assumed that the American air force would be able to carry out bombing raids on Japan from bases in China but the focus shifted when the United States decided to concentrate its efforts on taking the Japanese-held islands in the Pacific. The dropping of the atomic bombs on Hiroshima (6 August 1945) and Nagasaki (9 August 1945) brought the war to an abrupt end, with Japan announcing its surrender on 15 August 1945.

Barely twenty-four hours before the dropping of the second atomic bomb, the Soviet Union declared war on Japan and Russian troops poured into Manchuria. Stalin, in response to the urging of his western allies, had promised at Yalta in February 1945 that he would enter the war against Japan shortly after the defeat of Germany. The unexpected end to the war in Asia obviated the need for Soviet intervention, but Stalin went ahead anyway, especially as he had gained allied approval for the Soviet Union's 'pre-eminent interests' in Manchuria (Mancall, 1984, p. 297). On the day Japan surrendered, Stalin signed a thirty-year treaty of friendship with Chiang Kai-shek promising future Soviet withdrawal from Manchuria but also allowing the Soviet Union the use of Port Arthur and joint management of the Chinese Eastern Railway. As in the early 1920s the Soviet Union was playing a skilful 'double game'.

The end of the China war thus bequeathed a tense and complicated situation, with the presence of Russian troops in Manchuria and the race that quickly ensued between the communists and nationalists (aided by the United States) to accept the surrender of Japanese forces in China, most of which remained intact. Before discussing the civil war that resulted and the victory of the CCP, it is first necessary to describe communist policy in Yanan and the emergence of Mao Zedong as undisputed leader of the CCP.

The Yanan Period, 1937–45

After 1945 Mao was often wistfully to refer to the Yanan period as a time when close links were forged between the party and the people and when a spirit of egalitarianism prevailed in the struggle to overcome both the Japanese menace and the economic blockade imposed on Yanan by the Guomindang (Meisner, 1977, pp. 47–51). The Yanan period also witnessed Mao's final victory over the 'Internationalist faction' (those with close links to the Comintern, such as Wang Ming and Bo Gu) for leadership of the CCP. In the process Mao affirmed his *ideological* leadership of the party, which was to mark the beginnings of a personal cult (Wylie, 1980).

In accord with the United Front, the CCP after 1937 stressed national unity and halted its radical programme of land confiscation, although land belonging to those who had collaborated with the Japanese continued to be appropriated (Kataoka, 1974). In 1940 Mao wrote an important article entitled 'On New Democracy', which presented the CCP as a genuine *national* movement, leading an *alliance* of 'revolutionary classes' (the proletariat, peasantry, petty bourgeoisie and national bourgeoisie). The 'new democracy', as Mao put it, would complete the tasks of the 'bourgeois–democratic' revolution before ushering in the socialist stage (Wylie, 1980,pp. 119–21). As Kataoka (1974) notes, Mao's concept of 'new democracy' was meant to counter the 'urban revolutionary line' of Wang Ming, who saw the Second United Front as the means to reassert proletarian hegemony in the cities.

Official CCP policy during the Yanan period therefore sought to protect private enterprise and encourage non-CCP participation in administration, particularly at the grass-roots level (without however, compromising the CCP's leadership role), while land policy aimed at improving the economic situation of the poor peasants through a campaign of rent and interest reduction. In areas where tenants were compelled to hand over as much as 50 per cent of their crop in rent and where tenants and landowning peasants alike were victims of unscrupulous moneylenders and landlords who charged exorbitant rates of interest for any loans extended, this campaign had a significant impact in galvanizing peasant support (Gillin, 1964; Selden, 1971).

By 1940–1, however, Mao began to feel that a number of problems

50

needed to be urgently dealt with. The Shen-Gan-Ning base area had by now expanded to cover an area of twenty-three counties with a population of 1.5 million. At the same time membership of the CCP increased from 40,000 in 1937 to 800,000 in 1940 (Wylie, 1980, p. 164), due to the influx of large numbers of intellectuals and students from the cities, who had regarded Yanan as the centre of national resistance to Japan. An over-staffed bureaucracy, particularly at higher levels, had developed. For Mao, this had led to the evil of 'bureaucratism', which threatened to divorce officials from the needs and concerns of the people. Mao also expressed concern that the party itself lacked internal cohesion with higher-level cadres possessing a mainly urban and intellectual background and lower-level cadres coming mostly from local rural areas. Mao was also keen to eliminate all vestiges of what he called 'dogmatism' or 'formalism' within the party, by which he meant an inflexible and rigid approach to Marxist doctrine without taking into account the concrete Chinese situation. Mao's target was clearly the 'Internationalist' faction led by Wang Ming, although his criticisms were also levelled at the growing numbers of 'bookish' intellectuals in Yanan. These political and ideological problems were compounded by the worsening economic situation as a result of the Guomindang blockade.

In 1942–3 Mao launched a rectification campaign designed to 're-educate' cadres and combat the 'evils' of bureaucratism and formalism. Since Mao's own writings formed an important component of the study materials used (Compton, 1966), this campaign confirmed Mao's ideological leadership of the party. In particular, Mao stressed the importance of the 'Sinification of Marxism' (the creative adaptation of Marxism to Chinese conditions), a concept to which he had first referred in 1938 and which, according to a recent study (Wylie, 1980), owed much to the writings of Chen Boda. Chen, who was to become Mao's political secretary and Director of the China Problems Research Section at the CCP's Central Party School in Yanan, had insisted since the 1930s that Marxism had roots in the *Chinese* past (e.g. Chen noted that the fifth-century BC thinker Mo Zi had shown an awareness of the class struggle) and had condemned wholesale imitation from abroad. In promoting the 'Sinification of Marxism' Mao was not only attacking those in the party closely associated with the Comintern but also, ultimately, asserting his ideological independence from Moscow.

Mao's leadership of the party was formally recognized in 1943 when he was elected chairman of the Politburo and the Central Committee. The increasing prominence attached to Mao's writings was also accompanied by the emergence of a Maoist cult. As early as 1937 Mao's portrait, with a personal quotation, appeared in a party journal, while the first published collection of his writings appeared at the end of that year. In 1944 the first edition of Mao's

Selected Works was published and the new party constitution drawn up by the Seventh Party Congress (April–June 1945) noted that 'Mao's thought'(*Mao Zedong sixiang*) constituted the 'single ideological guide' for the CCP (Wylie,1980).

In the wake of the rectification campaign attempts were made to reduce the numbers of bureaucratic personnel; higher-level party cadres, administrators and intellectuals were encouraged to participate in manual labour at the local level, in what was called the 'to the village campaign' (*xiafang*). Army units, also, were meant to take part in agricultural production, particularly during the busy season. Rural part-time schools were set up to spread both literacy and practical skills. To counter the effects of the economic blockade, local, small-scale industry was promoted, involving peasant households (in particular, the women) in such things as weaving or iron-smelting. Overall, Mao stressed the importance of the 'mass line', the need for party cadres to remain in close touch with grass-roots opinion (Selden, 1971).

At the same time Mao called for closer supervision of administration by the party, reflecting his concern that co-ordination between the two was not sufficient. He also used the rectification campaign to urge the creation of a genuine 'revolutionary literature', criticizing the elitism of certain writers and intellectuals in Yanan. In his 'Talks at the Yanan Forum on Literature and Art' in 1942, Mao argued that intellectuals needed to have a deeper understanding of the 'masses' in order that their work might truly represent the 'proletarian standpoint'. In a sense, Mao's speech signalled the beginning of greater party control over intellectuals and a number of them, including Ding Ling, the noted woman writer, were criticized for the negative attitude they had taken towards the party (Ding Ling had been particularly critical of the lack of progress made in improving the situation of women).

Foreign visitors to Yanan throughout this period, however, consistently remarked upon the high morale and dedication shown by the communists. The American journalist, Edgar Snow, had first brought Mao and his colleagues to the world's attention when he visited Yanan in 1936 and then wrote his classic account of the CCP, *Red Star Over China* (1938), which depicted the communists as sincere revolutionaries. By 1944 American official interest in the CCP was sufficient to prompt the sending to Yanan of an army observer group, known as the Dixie Mission, under Colonel Barrett. Mao was keen to obtain American aid for the struggle against Japan, and in an interview in August 1944 with John Service, a foreign affairs officer attached to the Mission, Mao expressed his hope that Washington might mediate between Yanan and Chongqing. Later in the same year President Roosevelt sent his personal emissary, Patrick Hurley, to Yanan and a five-point draft programme was agreed as a basis for CCP–Guomindang reconciliation, including the formation of a coalition government and legal status for the CCP (Schaller, 1979; Reardon-Anderson, 1980). Chiang Kai-shek's unwillingness to accept the draft programme effectively put an end to any hopes of a *modus vivendi*.

Although Mao never did receive the American aid he had hoped for, by the time the war ended Yanan had considerably expanded its influence, controlling eighteen base areas (with a population of 100 million), mainly throughout north China.

4 The New Communist
    Government

The war against Japan had taken an enormous toll of the
Chinese people. Large areas of the country were devastated and
communications destroyed. Eight years of war had resulted in 1.5
million Chinese killed and almost 2 million wounded, while the
country's war debt had escalated to 1,464 billion Chinese dollars
(Hsü, 1983a, p. 611). All hopes, however, that peace and stability
might now prevail were cruelly dashed as increasing hostility between
Chiang Kai-Shek and the CCP, whose forces now totalled 1 million
regular troops and 2 million militia, erupted into a bloody civil war.

The Civil War

With the formal ending of the war there was an immediate rush to
accept the Japanese surrender and hence acquire their weapons.
Chiang issued orders that Japanese troops were to surrender only
to nationalist forces and even commanded that until then they be
responsible (along with former collaborators) for maintaining law and
order in the cities. Inevitably, this caused much resentment among
the urban population (Pepper, 1978). At the same time Chiang relied
on American assistance to airlift his troops to Beijing, Tianjin,
Nanjing and Shanghai. American marines also landed in north China
to await the arrival of nationalist troops (Schaller, 1979). Chiang's
attempt to take over the cities in Manchuria, however, was hindered
by the continued presence of Soviet troops in the region, despite
Stalin's promise that they would be withdrawn after the Japanese
surrender. By the time they did leave, in May 1946, taking with
them much of Manchuria's heavy industrial plant, worth an estimated
858 million US dollars (Mancall, 1984, p. 319), the communists
had succeeded in extending their control to most of the Manchurian
countryside.

By this time large-scale fighting had already broken out between
communist and nationalist forces. Although Mao had flown to
Chongqing in August 1945 to negotiate with Chiang, talks soon

broke down as Chiang insisted that communist troops be placed under nationalist control before he would consider Mao's demand for a coalition government. Chiang's intransigence was bolstered by his confidence in the United States' support although, ironically, the new American president, Harry Truman, who succeeded Roosevelt on his death in April 1945, was far more circumspect in his support for Chiang than his predecessor had been. In December 1945 Truman sent his special ambassador, General George Marshall, to China in order to act as mediator. A temporary ceasefire was arranged and a Political Consultative Conference convened, but co-operation proved impossible. With the renewal of fighting in April 1946 Chiang convened a Guomindang-dominated national assembly without CCP participation. Marshall returned to the United States in January 1947, his mediation attempt having totally failed. As Secretary of State after 1947 Marshall was to adopt a cautious policy with regard to China and even reduced financial aid to Chiang.

Chiang, however, was confident of success. His troops outnumbered those of the CCP and were also better equipped. In March 1947 the communists were even forced to evacuate Yanan. Yet the fatal flaws which had characterized the nationalist armies during the war against Japan continued to exist. They were poorly led and badly co-ordinated. Enforced recruitment of civilians and the undisciplined behaviour of the troops alienated growing numbers of the population. Conditions within the army itself were so brutal that desertion from the ranks was common.

At the same time areas under nationalist control experienced an accelerating rate of inflation and the currency virtually collapsed. Efforts to implement economic reform were consistently undermined by corruption within Guomindang ranks. Chiang himself remarked in January 1948 that 'never, in China or abroad, has there been a revolutionary party as decrepit and degenerate as we are today; nor has there been one as lacking in spirit, in discipline, and even more in standards of right and wrong as we are today' (Eastman, 1984, p. 203).

Manchuria, where Chiang had committed some of his best troops, was the first region to fall to the communists, in 1948. By early 1949 the garrisons at Beijing and Tianjin had surrendered wholesale. The United States became increasingly reluctant to bale Chiang out, although growing criticism from the administration's Republican opponents, some of whom formed an effective pressure group known as the China Lobby, compelled Truman in February 1948 to recommend a grant-in-aid of 570 million US dollars (less than Chiang had asked for). United States government policy satisfied no one. Chiang complained bitterly about the inadequate amount of American financial aid, but the very fact that Washington had extended such aid only served to reinforce the CCP's contention that the United

States was actively interfering in China's internal affairs. Furthermore, the Administration's domestic critics were to accuse the government (and, in particular, the State Department) of having 'betrayed' Chiang Kai-shek and hence of having 'lost' China (Tucker, 1983).

With CCP forces poised to take South China in April 1949 Stalin advised caution, and even suggested that partition might be a serious option. In line with current Soviet thinking, which divided the world into two hostile camps – the socialist and the imperialist – Stalin argued that nothing should be done which might provoke United States military intervention in China and hence involve the Soviet Union, as the centre of the socialist camp, in a world war. No doubt Stalin's advice also reflected his mixed feelings concerning the prospect of having a potential rival communist power as a near neighbour. Mao, however, insisted that it was precisely in the 'intermediate zone' (colonial and semi-colonial countries) that the imperialist camp could be defeated, thereby *avoiding* world war (Gittings, 1974; Yahuda, 1978). In any event, Mao, in 1946, had already dismissed the potential threat of American military and nuclear power as a 'paper tiger' that could be overcome by a 'people's war'. Mao's ignoring of Stalin's advice also showed that just as the Yanan period had witnessed an emphasis on 'self-reliance' (*zili gengsheng*) in the economic sphere, so too would Mao adhere to 'self-reliance' in foreign policy, an important contributory factor to the future Sino-Soviet dispute.

In October 1949, from the Gate of Heavenly Peace, Mao proclaimed the establishment of the People's Republic of China. By the end of the year the Guomindang government had retreated to Taiwan, from where it was to continue to insist that it represented the true 'Republic of China'. Although the United States rejected the possibility of protecting Taiwan militarily its relations with the new communist regime had deteriorated sufficiently for Washington to impose a trade embargo on Beijing (Tucker, 1983). Over the next few years, moreover, the United States was to associate itself more closely with the Taiwan regime, constituting for the new communist government direct interference in China's internal affairs (by preventing Taiwan's reunification with the mainland) and virtually ruling out meaningful relations between the two countries until the 1970s.

There has been much debate over the reasons for the communist victory in 1949. Johnson (1962) argues that is was essentially the war with Japan that brought the CCP to power because of its appeal to nationalism. A recent study of Manchuria from the 1920s to 1945 adopts a similar thesis and argues that it was not until the CCP actively encouraged and led a united anti-Japanese struggle that it was able to acquire a mass following (Chong-sik Lee, 1983). Other historians have stressed the CCP's social and economic policies, particularly the campaign to reduce land rent and interest on loans, as an important factor in mobilizing peasant support (Gillin, 1964; Selden, 1971). A first-hand account of changes in a Shanxi village during the late 1940s shows that the more radical policy (adopted in 1947) of confiscating land belonging to landlords and rich peasants and redistributing it to poorer peasants was a crucial factor in the CCP's final victory (Hinton, 1966).

Another study goes further and claims that it was only when the CCP adapted its policies to the needs and aspirations of the peasants themselves that it gained a widespread following (Thaxton, 1983). A recent article asserts, however, that the support of the peasantry did not necessarily guarantee the victory of the CCP and that it was the prudent attitude taken towards the rural elites and petty bourgeoisie during the Yanan period and after which ensured there would be no effective opposition to the CCP (Shum, 1985).

Pepper (1978) and Eastman (1984) focus their attention on the disintegration and internal collapse of the Guomindang itself. Pepper shows how the Guomindang progressively alienated students, intellectuals and urban bourgeoisie through its determination to prosecute an unpopular civil war and its failure to stem economic collapse in the cities or stamp out corruption amongst officialdom. Eastman argues that the peasantry in nationalist-controlled areas, as a result of forced labour and military conscription and burdensome taxes, simply withdrew their support from the regime, although disillusionment with the government had evidently set in well before the late 1940s, as a recent anthology of letters and articles written in 1936 testifies (Cochran and Hsieh, 1983, pp. 71–137).

In any event, the proclamation of the People's Republic in October 1949 marked the end of the turbulent quest since 1912 to create a unified nation state, an ambition achieved by a communist revolution that had been overwhelmingly rural in origin. After more than twenty years of revolutionary struggle, the CCP now faced the daunting task of administering the entire country.

The People's Democratic Dictatorship

On the eve of the communist victory, Mao wrote an important article entitled 'On the People's Democratic Dictatorship', in which he set forth the aims of the future communist government. In line with his concept of 'New Democracy' Mao claimed that the CCP was leading an alliance of four classes (proletariat, peasantry, petty bourgeoisie and national bourgeoisie), all of which were to enjoy democratic rights and freedoms. This communist-led alliance would exercise 'dictatorship' over what Mao assumed to be a minority of counter revolutionaries, former Guomindang members, comprador bourgeoisie (i.e. those who had worked for, or were linked with, foreign economic interests) and landlords (Meisner, 1977; Brugger, 1981a).

Shortly after Mao wrote this article, in September 1949, he convened a Chinese People's Political Consultative Conference (CPPCC) in Beijing, in which a large number of non-CCP personalities participated. A Common Programme was drawn up which announced the elimination of all foreign privileges and property, and the confiscation of Guomindang capital; at the same time the Common Programme called for the implementation of land and marriage reform and envisaged a transitional period to socialism during which the private urban economy would continue to exist. Non-CCP members also participated in the new government, with several being appointed to the Government Administrative Council (under Zhou Enlai); furthermore, three of the six vice-chairmen of the People's Republic were non-communists.

Nevertheless, it was made clear that leadership was to be in the hands of the CCP. Until 1954, in fact, China was divided into six military-administrative regions (under the control of the various communist front armies), and it was a measure of the speed with which the party imposed centralized control that it was able to dismantle these regional administrations and replace them with district and provincial governments under the direct control of the centre. A State Constitution was also promulgated in 1954, which allowed for the creation of Peoples' Congresses at the local, provincial and central levels, the last one to be called the National People's Congress. Only the 'basic level' congresses were to be directly elected (under close CCP supervision), the membership of the higher congresses being nominated by the congress immediately below. Although in theory the People's Congresses were to oversee the administration at the equivalent level they were primarily used to provide a platform for official CCP policy. The CCP ensured overall control by creating party committees to supervise each level of administration (very often there was an overlap of personnel), while at the centre the CCP's Politburo (and, in particular, its five-man standing committee) wielded decisive influence over the formal government structure, which now comprised a State Council and a host of ministries. Here, too, an overlap of personnel was evident, the most obvious examples being that of Mao, who was concurrently president of the Republic and chairman of the CCP, and Zhou Enlai, who was both state premier (i.e. head of the State Council) and a member of the Politburo Standing Committee (Townsend, 1967; Saich, 1981).

High on the agenda of the new communist government was the completion of land reform, a process already begun after 1945 in those areas under communist control and one which involved the confiscation of land belonging to landlords and its redistribution to poor peasants. In some areas, particularly in 1947–8, the process had quickly got out of hand, leading to what was called 'leftist deviations', with rich peasants, as well as landlords, being attacked. The Agrarian Reform Law of June 1950 aimed to extend land reform to the whole country and to set limits on its targets. Only the land and property owned by landlords (comprising 4 per cent of the rural population and owning 30 per cent of the land) were to be confiscated and redistributed (although land owned for industrial and commercial enterprises was left intact, in line with the official policy of protecting the private industrial sector). Middling and rich peasants were specifically protected, and rich peasants could even rent out land providing it did not exceed the amount they tilled themselves.

The impact of land reform, however, was dramatic enough. Not only did it result in a large increase in the number of small peasant landholders, but it also ensured the elimination of the social and political influence of the rural elite. Peasant associations organized mass rallies during which individual peasants were encouraged to confront landlords and publicly denounce them. These 'speak bitterness' meetings, as they were called, led not only to the public humiliation of landlords but, in many cases, their execution as well. Land reform was completed by 1952 (Wong, 1973; Shue, 1980).

Another early priority of the new government was the implementation of marriage reform (Yang, 1959). A marriage reform law was promulgated in 1950 and was designed to end the traditional practice of arranged marriages and to allow free choice of marriage partners. Freedom of divorce was also granted. By insisting that all marriages henceforth had to be registered with the communist authorities, the government hoped to shift the focus of loyalty from the family to the state. Although marriage reform was considered as part of a wider campaign to bring about equality between the sexes, recent studies have shown that patriarchal attitudes still persist, not only amongst the population at large (particularly in the rural areas) but also within the party itself (Andors, 1983; Johnson, 1983; Stacey, 1983).

Mass campaigns were also organized in the cities, where the government was determined to stamp out all vestiges of corruption within the bureaucracy (many administrators from the previous regime remained in place, simply because the CCP lacked the personnel to take over from them) and in economic enterprises. Other aspects of urban life such as gambling, drug trafficking and prostitution (which Mao referred to as 'sugar-coated bullets' that might tempt unsuspecting party cadres as they entered the cities) were also strictly proscribed. Studies of individual cities such as Guangzhou, Tianjin and Shanghai have shown how successful the communists were in achieving these aims (Vogel, 1969; Lieberthal, 1980; Gaulton, 1981).

While private enterprise in the cities was initally protected, a gradual process of nationalization began in 1953 and was completed in 1956. At the same time the new government launched its first

Five Year Plan, which emphasized the promotion of heavy industry. In this China relied heavily on the support of the Soviet Union. Although Mao had stated in his article on the People's Democratic Dictatorship that the new government would be prepared to deal with any country on the basis of mutual respect for sovereignty, he also admitted that China needed 'to lean to one side' (i.e. towards the socialist camp headed by the Soviet Union). In any event, increasing American hostility, illustrated by Washington's imposition of a trade embargo on the People's Republic in November 1949, inevitably forced Mao to look to the Soviet Union for economic assistance.

Mao therefore went to Moscow between December 1949 and February 1950 and concluded a thirty-year alliance with the Soviet Union. Moscow promised to come to China's aid in the event of an attack on her by 'Japan or any other state which should unite in any form with Japan in acts of aggression' (a clear reference to the United States). Moscow also agreed to extend a fixed credit worth 300 million US dollars (repayable at 1 per cent interest per annum) with which to purchase Soviet machinery and equipment. Further credits were to be extended in 1954. At the same time Stalin secured a number of concessions from Mao that included recognition of the Soviet Union's rights in southern Manchuria originally granted by Chiang Kai-shek in his 1945 treaty with Stalin (i.e. continued Russian naval use of Lushun, formerly Port Arthur, and Dairen), continued joint Sino-Russian administration of the Chinese Eastern Railway, and Beijings recognition of the independence of Outer Mongolia (now within the Soviet Union's sphere of influence). Later agreements also provided for the creation of Sino-Soviet joint stock companies to exploit mineral resources in Xinjiang as well as to run a number of civil airline routes. Although by 1954 Moscow had returned Lushun, Dairen and the Chinese Eastern Railway to sole Chinese control and had sold its shares in the joint stock companies, the very fact that Mao had been obliged to grant these concessions in the first place had been a great shock and he was later to refer bitterly to the arduous negotiations of 1950.

It is with this in mind that Mancall (1984, p. 368) describes the Sino-Soviet Alliance as an 'unequal relationship' but it is important to remember the benefits that China gained from it. First, the alliance provided a nuclear umbrella for China at a time when relations with the United States were extremely tense. In 1950 the invasion of South Korea by communist North Korea (Korea had been partitioned in 1945) prompted the intervention of United Nations forces, mainly comprising American troops, under General MacArthur. When UN forces in turn went on the offensive and advanced deep into North Korean territory, almost as far as the Sino-Korean border, Beijing sent 'volunteers' in October 1950 to participate in the fighting on the North Korean side (Whiting, 1960). A war of attrition followed, ended by an armistice in 1953 that settled virtually on the original line of demarcation between the two Koreas – the 38th parallel. The Sino-Soviet Alliance may very well have been a factor in deterring a direct American attack on China, although, it should be noted, Soviet material assistance to China during the war was minimal and arrived late on in the proceedings.

Second, the Sino-Soviet Alliance paved the way for Soviet assistance in China's first Five Year Plan. Moscow contributed to the construction of over 100 industrial plants in machine-building, metallurgy, coal, iron and steel, and sent thousands of experts to offer advice and help with training. At the same time Chinese students were sent to the Soviet Union. Overall, the early 1950s witnessed considerable Soviet influence in China. Soviet textbooks and technical manuals were translated wholesale into Chinese and used extensively in education. Furthermore, the first Five Year Plan was based very much on the Soviet model, with an emphasis on both heavy industry and centralized planning.

The Sino-Soviet relationship, however, was fraught with potential tension. During the course of the 1950s Mao became increasingly dissatisfied not only with the Soviet model of economic development (see chapter 5) but also with Moscow's attempt to exert control over China's defence and foreign policies, in particular its reluctance to share nuclear technology with Beijing and its lukewarm support of Beijing's campaign to retrieve Taiwan, now linked to the United States by a 1954 defence treaty (Yahuda, 1978). It is significant that the first crisis within the CCP leadership, in 1953, involved the condemnation and purge of Gao Gang, head of the party apparatus in Manchuria and of the newly created State Planning Commission. Gao was known to have had close ties with Moscow and was accused of attempting to set up an 'independent kingdom' in the north-east (Meisner, 1977, pp. 131–3; Brugger, 1981a, pp. 101–3).

Collectivization and the Hundred Flowers

Since the principal domestic source of finance for industrialization was to be the agricultural sector, it was hoped that land reform would lead to increased production in the countryside. At the same time a gradual process of collectivization was envisaged, beginning with the formation of mutual aid teams and ultimately ending with the creation of 'higher agricultural producers' co-operatives' (APCs), when private ownership of land would be eliminated. The first Five Year Plan, for example, originally set a target suggesting that by 1957 one-third of peasant households would join lower APCs, in which land, although still privately owned, would be pooled and farmed collectively.

61

Burdened by heavy state taxes and its efficiency hampered by the fragmentation of landholdings, the agricultural sector did not achieve the hoped-for increase in production. Poorer peasants, always at a disadvantage because of the lack of appropriate credit facilities and their inability to purchase modern equipment, quickly became indebted to their richer neighbours, often losing their land in the process. Mao began to fear the restoration of exploitative class relations in the countryside and referred to the emergence of a 'new rich peasant class'. Although the Central Committee called for a speeding-up of collectivization in mid-1955, Mao was still not satisfied and in July 1955, in a speech addressed to a meeting of provincial and regional party secretaries, he criticized the party's caution in the wake of 'spontaneous' enthusiasm for collectivization amongst the peasants themselves and called for the schedule to be brought forward, declaring that one-half of all peasant households should join lower APCs by early 1958. This was the first, although certainly not the last, time that Mao went over the heads of his colleagues in the Politburo to appeal to a wider audience. He implicitly rejected the view held by many of the 'planners' in the CCP leadership, including the vice-chairman of the party, Liu Shaoqi, that the socialization of agriculture was dependent on the prior development of industry and extensive mechanization in the countryside. For Mao the very process of collectivization itself would stimulate mass enthusiasm and hence lead to increased production.

Ironically, even Mao's target was quickly overtaken during the winter of 1955–6 as the movement took on a momentum of its own. By mid-1956 virtually all peasant households had been organized into lower APCs and the final stage of collectivization was then completed soon afterwards when most lower APCs were transformed into higher APCs in the spring of 1957. Although higher APCs, initially comprising about 250 households but later reduced to 150, ended the households' individual ownership of land, private plots were permitted, principally for domestic use (Meisner, 1977, pp. 140–60).

Mao also moved decisively in launching a campaign to combat bureaucratism within the party. Mao's concern over this dated from the Yanan period, but for Mao the problem had become especially serious during the first years of the new government, with the proliferation of central government ministries and commissions, and the growth of a party bureaucracy increasingly differentiated by elaborate grade and salary scales (Harding, 1981). It is significant that the lesson Mao drew from Khrushchev's secret speech of February 1956 denouncing Stalin's crimes was that communist parties had to beware of alienating the people. Proclaiming the slogan 'Let a hundred flowers blossom and a hundred schools of thought contend', Mao called on the non-party intelligensia to offer criticisms of the party so that it might be revitalized. This 'open-door rectification', as Mao termed it, did not meet with the approval of many of Mao's colleagues who, although quite willing to agree to criticisms made of party bureaucrats 'behind closed doors', were not happy to see such a process extended beyond the party. Intellectuals, themselves, were initially cautious but criticisms began to appear in the press during the summer of 1956.

The party's lukewarm reaction to Mao's initiative was clearly shown at the Eighth Party Congress in September 1956, when mere formal approval was given. The implicit condemnation of 'personality cults' contained in Khrushchev's secret speech also made Mao's position vulnerable. The reference to 'Mao Zedong Thought' was deleted from the new party constitution, while the post of party secretary-general was revived and awarded to Deng Xiaoping who, like Liu Shaoqi, was unenthusiastic about 'open-door rectification'. Riots in Poland and the anti-Stalinist revolution in Hungary during the latter half of 1956 only confirmed fears of what might happen if the party lowered its guard.

Mao revived the debate in February 1957 in a speech entitled 'On the Correct Handling of Contradictions Among the People', which he addressed to a Supreme State Conference (therefore once again bypassing the party leadership). Mao argued that unless the party was willing to listen to criticisms from outside, a non-antagonistic contradiction between the party and the people could be transformed into an antagonistic one, a bold statement to make for someone who was a communist party chairman (MacFarquhar, 1974). Again, after initial timidity, intellectuals and students began to voice their criticisms in the summer of 1957. On university campuses students displayed 'big character posters' (*dazibao*) accusing party cadres of becoming a new elite; they were arrogant and insensitive to the people's needs. Some intellectuals even went so far as to criticize one-party rule and to question the validity of socialism itself (MacFarquhar, 1960).

The ferocity of the criticism took Mao by surprise, as he had assumed that the intelligentsia was united in its general sympathy for socialism. He was now forced to retreat from his original position (no doubt encouraged by his colleagues) and in June 1957 a revised version of his February speech was published, which defined 'correct criticism' as that which strengthened party leadership and upheld the socialist system. Intellectuals were condemned as 'poisonous weeds' and subjected to criticism in an anti-rightist campaign, which involved many of them having to undergo labour reform.

Although the Hundred Flowers campaign had failed as far as Mao was concerned, the growing dissatisfaction he felt with the way the party was developing (which had led him to launch the campaign in the first place), as well as with the Soviet model of economic development that the first Five Year Plan had adopted, prompted Mao to change direction in 1958.

5 Mao Attempts to Steer a New Course

Mao had questioned the Soviet model as early as 1956. In a speech entitled 'On the Ten Great Relationships' (details of which were only known a decade later) Mao called for an emphasis on light industry and agriculture, the industrialization of the countryside, the decentralization of planning, the priority of labour-intensive projects over capital-intensive ones, the development of inland areas (away from the coastal areas) and the replacement of material incentives with moral incentives (Schram, 1974, pp. 61–83). This collection of strategies, in Mao's view, would lead to rapid economic development and allow China to overtake the capitalist West.

The Great Leap Forward

The slogan 'Great Leap Forward' was first used at the end of 1957 in connection with a water conservancy campaign that had required greater mobilization of manpower than that provided by the higher APCs. However, the slogan soon began to take on a much wider meaning, reflecting Mao's boundless confidence that radical social, economic and ideological transformation would lead not only to a communist society but also to a rapid increase in industrial production (Meisner, 1977, pp. 204–25). As in 1955, Mao would insist that social and ideological change was the prerequisite, rather than the result, of economic development. At Politburo meetings during the first months of 1958 Mao outlined his plans with the call to 'go all out, aim high, and achieve greater, faster, better and more economical results' (MacFarquhar, 1983, p. 42).

In this he was supported by the 'planners' in the party hierarchy such as vice-chairman Liu Shaoqi, who had confidently predicted at the end of 1957 that China would surpass the United Kingdom in the production of iron, steel and other industrial products (Schram, 1973; MacFarquhar, 1983, p. 17). MacFarquhar (1983, p. 54), however, also points out that there was a difference in *approach*, with Liu stressing the need for the masses' enthusiasm to be harnessed and guided by the party leadership whereas Mao, as we shall see, saw the Great Leap as a means to 'unleash' the masses. The Second Five Year Plan (due to start in 1958) was virtually scrapped as provincial cadres, taking their cue from the ambitious statements publicized by the central leadership, substantially revised output figures upwards. In Guangdong province, for example, the planned increase in industrial production for 1958 had been set at 5.8 per cent in October 1957. By early February 1958 the planned increased was revised upwards to 33.2 per cent (Brugger, 1981a, p. 182).

Economically, it was hoped that the Great Leap would reduce the gap between city and countryside by promoting the development of small-scale industry, such as crop-processing and tool manufacture, in the rural areas. Labour-intensive projects, in particular, would utilize China's one advantage – a surplus of manpower – and thereby eliminate both under-employment in the countryside and unemployment in the cities (caused by migrations from the rural areas). Mao's voluntaristic faith in the potential of mass mobilization was well illustrated in his description of China as 'poor and blank', which he saw as positive attributes because there would be more scope for development.

Mao argued that in the process of industrializing the countryside the masses themselves would master technology and thereby reduce their dependence on a technological elite, the emergence of which Mao saw as an inevitable consequence of the Soviet-inspired first Five Year Plan. In a wider sense, the Great Leap would promote self-reliance (*zili gengsheng*) and hence assert China's independence *vis-à-vis* the Soviet Union. The following two complaints raised by Mao at a party conference in Chengdu, in March 1958, provide revealing testimony to his dissatisfaction with the Sino-Soviet relationship.

First, having complained that China had imported foreign (i.e. Soviet) methods, even in the realm of education, Mao continued:

> The same applied to our public health work with the result that I could not have eggs or chicken soup for three years because an article appeared in the Soviet Union which said that one should not eat them... We lacked understanding of the whole economic situation and understood still less the differences between the Soviet Union and China. So all we could do was follow blindly. (Meisner, 1977, pp. 223–4)

Second, Mao referred to the unequal nature of the Sino-Soviet relationship by noting that:

> Chinese people used to be slaves and it appeared that they would continue that way. Whenever a Chinese artist painted a picture of me with Stalin, I was always shown shorter than Stalin (MacFarquhar, 1983, p. 38)

In order to modify the structure of centralized planning that had emerged in the early 1950s, the Great Leap also involved decentralization. By June 1959 80 per cent of central government enterprises were under provincial control while, at the same time, the number of central government ministries was reduced from 41 in 1957 to 30 in 1959 (MacFarquhar, 1983, pp. 59–60). Adopting Schurmann's (1968, pp. 175–6) useful distinction between decentralization which transfers decision-making power to the production units themselves ('decentralization I') and decentralization which transfers decision-making power only to some lower level of regional administration ('decentralization II'), the Great Leap implemented the latter. More importantly, however, such a decentralization gave the party more control over the economy since it was the provincial *party committees* that supervised economic enterprises and performed a co-ordinating role, thereby further reducing the influence of the central planning ministries. Greater party control was necessary, Mao argued, because ideological soundness was just as, if not more, important than technical expertise. Hence cadres were expected to be both 'red' and 'expert', while it was clearly stated that 'politics are in command'.

The symbol of the Great Leap was the commune. In December 1957 Mao had called for an amalgamation of collectives to facilitate the mobilization of larger groups of people for water conservancy work. By April 1958 an experimental commune was formed in Henan, followed by others in Hebei and the north-east. Mao encouraged this development, although it was not until July 1958 that the word 'commune' (*renmin gongshe*) appeared in a party publication and not until August 1958 that the party formally ratified the creation of communes at the Beidaihe conference, noting that they marked the transition stage to full communism. By September 1958, 90 per cent of the peasant population were organized into communes, each one comprising an average total of 5,000 households (30,000 people).

The communes, possessing political, social and economic functions, were not only to promote the 'industrialization' of the countryside, but also to help lessen the gap between urban and rural areas by encouraging the expansion of rural part-time schools and clinics. Since modern hospitals and western-trained doctors were generally concentrated in the towns and cities, increased use was also made of 'barefoot doctors', mobile personnel with a training in Chinese traditional medicine, to ensure that health care was enjoyed by the more remote rural areas. The very distinction between mental and manual labour was also to be eliminated with the creation of commune-funded half-work, half-study schools. Thousands of students and intellectuals were 'sent down' to the countryside to live among the peasants and participate in production work, although a recent study has shown that peasants did not always view these 'outsiders' positively, while many students themselves were resentful at having had to forego a comfortable urban education (Bernstein, 1977).

Another function assigned to the commune was the formation of a people's militia and the slogan 'everyone a soldier' was publicized with particular fervour in July–August 1958 since this was a period of increasing tension with the United States over the Taiwan issue (Yahuda, 1978, pp. 106–7). In a wider sense, Mao's enthusiasm for a people's militia revealed a difference in emphasis from that of the defence minister, Peng Dehuai. As MacFarquhar (1983, p 14) points out, while Mao was keen to develop nuclear weapons so that China could both play an independent world role and reduce its dependence on a professionalized army (relying more on a people's militia and using surplus funds for industrialization), Peng Dehuai preferred to rely on the Soviet nuclear shield so that China could build up a modernized and highly professional army. Peng may not have been over-enthusiastic, for example, about Mao's insistence that officers in the regular army, the People's Liberation Army (PLA), spend time in the ranks as ordinary soldiers or that the role of political commissars within the army be enhanced.

Meanwhile, by the end of 1958, it became apparent that the Great Leap had generated serious problems. Despite the relative moderation of the party's Beidaihe resolution in August 1958 ratifying the creation of communes (for example, the size of the commune was not to exceed 2,000 households; the arrival of communism was still described as a long-term eventuality; cadres were to exercise restraint in their dealings with the peasants), there was a frenzied rush by commune administrators to usher in the communist utopia, which only succeeded in antagonizing large numbers of peasants. Peasants were compelled to eat in communal mess halls as part of an effort to reduce the importance of the family unit. Household goods and property were confiscated; in connection with the 'backyard steel production' campaign (involving the use of makeshift steel furnaces), for example, even cooking utensils were appropriated by the commune. Large-scale construction projects took peasants away from crucial agricultural work. The transportation system was inadequate to meet the demands made of it and it was not uncommon for food supplies to rot as priority was given to the transportation of steel and other products.

Furthermore, organizational chaos abounded as local cadres competed with each other in the frequent raising of unrealistic output quotas. In this they took their cue from the centre. In August 1958, for example, the steel target was set at 10.7 million tons (double the 1957 output); the previous February it had been raised to 6.2 million tons and in May to 8.5 million tons (MacFarquhar, 1983, pp. 85,

67

89). Mao himself had confidently predicted that by 1960 China would be the world's third largest steel producer.

Amidst growing food shortages, party leaders met at Wuhan in December 1958 and called for moderation. They stressed once again the long-term achievement of communism and criticized 'commandism' (i.e. imposition of measures without duly consulting the desires of the masses). Individual ownership of personal goods was restored and households were once again to enjoy the use of private plots. The principle of distribution according to work was reaffirmed in criticism of those communes that had attempted to implement a 'free supply system'. It was at the Wuhan plenum that Mao confirmed an earlier decision he had made to step down as chairman of the Republic. Liu Shaoqi was formally to replace him in April 1959. Although Mao retained the chairmanship of the party he was later to complain that he was increasingly ignored when important decisions were made, accusing his colleagues (in particular Liu Shaoqi and Deng Xiaoping) of treating him 'like a dead ancestor'.

The food shortages were exacerbated by natural disasters in 1959 and 1960, with drought affecting large areas of north China and floods devastating southern China. Recent reports from China suggest that between 15 and 30 million people died during these years as a result of widespread famine (MacFarquhar, 1983, p. 330). At the Lushan (Jiangxi province) plenum in July–August 1959 Peng Dehuai sternly criticized the follies of the Great Leap. Mao, viewing Peng's criticism as a questioning of the entire Great Leap strategy, denounced Peng for breaking party ranks and accused him of leading an 'anti-party clique'. Other party leaders supported Mao; after all, Liu Shaoqi himself had initially been an enthusiastic supporter of the Great Leap.

Peng's case was not helped by the fact that his criticism coincided with increasing condemnation of the Great Leap by Soviet leaders. Already before 1958 serious ideological differences had arisen with the Soviet Union over Khrushchev's espousal of 'peaceful coexistence' with the capitalist world and what Mao regarded as Moscow's lukewarm support for national wars of liberation. Another source of disagreement concerned Beijing's insistence that communist parties work together on an equal basis rather than automatically accept Moscow's leadership in doctrinal and strategic matters. In July 1958 Khrushchev had visited Beijing and had further antagonized Mao with his suggestion that the two countries enter into joint military arrangements, which would have restricted Beijing's freedom of manoeuvre. Khrushchev was also reluctant fully to support Beijing in its dispute with the United States over Taiwan, seeing Beijing's threat to bombard the offshore islands (under nationalist control) as dangerous 'brinkmanship'.

By 1959 Khruschev was openly criticizing the communes and

belittled Beijing's claims that China had entered the transitional stage to communism. In the same year he scrapped the nuclear agreement signed in 1957, which had promised Soviet assistance for China's nuclear weapons programme, and in 1960 withdrew all Soviet advisers and experts from China. Over 200 co-operative projects had to be abandoned. From 1960 onwards both sides publicly attacked each other and, with the signing of the Test Ban Treaty by the Soviet Union, the United States and Britain in 1962, Beijing formally announced its intention to 'go its own way' in international affairs (Zagoria, 1962; Gittings, 1968; Yahuda, 1978).

Although the party leadership had closed ranks behind Mao in his confrontation with Peng Dehuai, the Great Leap itself was formally ended in 1960 and in the ensuing years Mao was compelled to witness a retreat from Great Leap policies as Liu Shaoqi and Deng Xiaoping sought to reassert centralized control and implement more pragmatic economic measures.

The Cultural Revolution

After 1960, Liu Shaoqi and Deng Xiaoping proceeded to reverse many Great Leap policies, in what Meisner (1977) describes as the 'Thermidorean Reaction'. Bureaucratic control from the centre was restored. The socio-economic functions of the communes were reduced and the production team (coinciding with the natural village) was made the basic production and accounting unit. Private plots and free rural markets were tolerated. Many rural part-time schools and clinics were closed down as resources were once again shifted in favour of urban areas. There was a general tendency to play down the importance of ideological campaigns as emphasis was now placed on expertise (as opposed to 'redness') and economic recovery. The pragmatic atmosphere of the time was well illustrated by a remark attributed to Deng Xiaoping; 'What does it matter if the cat is white or black, as long as it catches mice.'

In 1962 Mao first began to voice his fears of a 'restoration' of reactionary classes, arguing that even in a socialist society 'bourgeois elements' might emerge. More importantly, by September 1962 Mao was calling for class struggle against 'revisionism' – the appearance of bourgeois elements *within* the party itself. Mao pointed to the example of the Soviet Union, whose foreign policy proved that its leadership was 'revisionist'.

Mao hoped to restore his own influence and combat 'revisionist tendencies' through two campaigns that were promoted in the early 1960s. In 1963 Lin Biao, who had succeeded Peng Dehuai as defence minister in 1958 and was a Mao supporter, launched the 'Learn from the PLA' campaign (Gittings, 1967). The army was portrayed as the model of socialist virtues, whose example the people were to emulate. Regular political study sessions became a feature of the soldiers' routines; it was during this campaign that the ubiquitous 'little red book' was compiled and published – an anthology of pithy sayings taken from Mao's speeches and articles. Individual soldiers, such as Lei Feng, were praised for their conscientious study of Mao's thought and for their selfless and tireless devotion to the people and to socialism.

Mao also hoped to revive ideological fervour with the Socialist Education Movement (1962–5), which aimed to correct 'unhealthy tendencies' in the countryside amongst both cadres and masses. These included too much attention being paid to private plots at the expense of the collective, and corruption amongst cadres (for example, acceptance of bribes and embezzling of accounts). Mao wanted to revive poor and lower-middle peasant associations so that they could play an important role in the supervision of cadres' work (and, in the process, to mobilize peasants behind socialist goals), but as a study of the movement shows (Baum, 1975), Liu Shaoqi and Deng Xiaoping preferred to send party-controlled 'work teams' from outside to criticize and supervise cadres. Mao's colleagues, in fact, blunted the impact of the movement and transformed it into a mere party-imposed and controlled rectification of errant cadres. Mao's frustration over the way in which the movement had been restricted was clearly shown in 1965 when he ominously referred to 'those people in positions of authority within the party who take the capitalist road' (Meisner, 1977, p. 292).

Mao's fear of 'revisionism' was compounded by two other factors. First, there was his concern, first voiced in 1964, over 'revolutionary successors'. Since even the Soviet leadership was plainly revisionist, was it not possible, Mao wondered, that China's younger generation, born after 1949 and thus having no personal experience of the arduous struggle to achieve liberation, would lose sight of the socialist ideas the party had fought for? It is no coincidence that it was precisely at this time that Mao launched a scathing attack on the education system, with its emphasis on academic achievement (neglecting ideological correctness as a criterion for advancement) and book-learning divorced from productive labour (Price, 1970, 1977; Chen, 1974, 1981).

Second, Mao became dissatisfied with developments in the cultural sphere. Not only had satirical articles appeared in 1961–2 criticizing the Great Leap (some of which, notably by the writer and Beijing Party Committee member Deng To, were thinly veiled attacks on Mao himself) but various views put forward by party intellectuals and writers seemed to question Maoist belief in the necessity for continued class struggle and radical ideological transformation. Historians and philosophers, for example, played down the importance of class struggle in Chinese history and affirmed the universal and timeless value of certain Confucian beliefs; they equated the Confucian concept of *jen* (compassionate benevolence) with humanism and asserted that it had no class nature. In the literary field, writers stressed the importance of 'middle characters', as opposed to portraying characters who were all good or all bad (Goldman, 1973). To Mao this was a dangerous manifestation of ideological neutrality.

In 1964 Mao called for a 'rectification' in the cultural domain, but once again he found himself thwarted by his party colleagues. A five-man party group was set up under Peng Zhen (head of the Beijing Party Committee and close associate of Liu Shaoqi) to investigate erroneous views, but its activities were limited and the rectification Mao had called for petered out at the end of 1965. This was not surprising since many of the party intellectuals who had aired their views in the early 1960s had close links with, or worked for, the Beijing Party Committee, and hence must have had at least the unofficial support of both Peng Zhen and Liu Shaoqi. One result of this brief 'rectification' was the public emergence of Mao's wife, Jiang Qing, who launched a campaign both to reform traditional Beijing opera and to produce 'revolutionary opera' that would accurately portray the heroic struggles of the party and its individual members to achieve liberation in 1949.

It was evidently at this point that Mao decided to launch a frontal assault on the party itself, which was to become known as the Great Proletarian Cultural Revolution. It began innocuously enough, with an article written by Yao Wenyuan, editor of the Shanghai *Cultural Daily*, which criticized a play written five years earlier by Wu Han (historian and vice-mayor of Beijing) entitled 'Hai Jui Dismissed from Office'. The play concerned the efforts of a local official to protect the peasants from rapacious gentry and landlords and how vested interests at court ensured his dismissal by the emperor. Yao claimed that the play was an attack on Mao since the emperor's dismissal of Hai Jui was an allegory for Mao's arbitrary dismissal of Peng Dehuai in 1959 for having opposed the communes. Yao declared that such a work was typical of the current revisionist line in the cultural domain and urged a more widespread rectification campaign.

Yao's reference to a seemingly innocuous historical play shows how political debate in China is often carried out in the form of historical allegories and allusions to the past, which serve to reflect views on current issues or problems. A recent study of Chinese intellectuals (Goldman, 1981) shows that between 1960 and 1976 the Maoists and their opponents recruited writers to their cause and that a vigorous philosophical and ideological debate occurred (at a time when free intellectual activity was being suppressed), often in the shape of obscure and seemingly harmless articles on past Chinese history. Goldman also distinguishes between the two groups of intellectuals. Writers such as Wu Han, who had the backing of the party bureaucracy, tended to be of an older generation and more cosmopolitan. Goldman compares them to the May Fourth liberals since they believed in both change and flexibility. The writers who were associated with Maoist policies were of a younger generation and less cosmopolitan, and Goldman likens them to a group of late-nineteenth-century Chinese officials, known as the *qingyi* (pure speech) faction, who had argued for a revival and strengthening of fundamental Confucian principles in the wake of the western military threat. In the same way, Maoist writers were urging a return to fundamental socialist principles.

Following Yao Wenyuan's article, attacks on Wu Han and other party intellectuals considered to be critics of the Maoist line became more common. In May 1966 Mao, in the name of the Central Committee (and with the support of Lin Biao and the PLA) dissolved Peng Zhen's five-man group and replaced it with his own Cultural Revolution group under the direction of Chen Boda and Jiang Qing. The Beijing Party Committee and government were also purged and Peng Zhen, Wu Han's patron, was dismissed. Liu Shaoqi's position was becoming increasingly vulnerable.

Mao now encouraged spontaneous struggle against all forms of bureaucratic authority. The first of such 'struggles' occurred at Beijing University where students denounced university administrators in May–June 1966 for having attempted to dampen the students' political enthusiasm and deflect criticism of Wu Han (Nee, 1969). In June 1966 it was announced that university entrance examinations would be postponed for six months while the education system was being reconstructed. With such slogans as 'to rebel is justified' (*zaofan you daoli*), students increasingly took to the streets criticizing teachers, intellectuals, and government and party cadres. From out of these demonstrations (and struggles amongst the students themselves) emerged the Red Guards, high-school and university students who saw themselves as the genuine upholders of Mao's thought. Mao welcomed these developments. In his view youth would gain a unique opportunity to experience revolution by participating in 'struggles' against those in authority and hence earn the right to acquire the title of 'revolutionary successors'.

At a Central Committee Meeting in August 1966 packed with Mao supporters, a sixteen-point programme was outlined to define the aims of the Cultural Revolution. Not only was it to overthrow 'those within the party who are in authority taking the capitalist road' but it was also to destroy the 'four olds' – old ideas, old culture, old customs and old habits. Mao was aiming at nothing less than a total transformation of people's thought and behaviour. Liu Shaoqi and Deng Xiaoping disappeared from public view after November 1966 (Liu was formally expelled from the party in 1968) and Lin Biao emerged as Mao's 'closest comrade in arms' and his appointed successor. Shortly after the August meeting of the Central Committee, Mao met with thousands of Red Guards in Beijing and their frenzied adulation of Mao and his thought now attained fanatical proportions. With schools and universities closed until further notice, Red Guards were encouraged to travel around the country exchanging revolutionary experiences and to 'bombard the headquarters' of local and regional party organizations.

Interpretations of the Cultural Revolution vary. Some have adopted a psychoanalytical approach. Thus, for example, Lifton (1968) argues that the Cultural Revolution was the vehicle for the promotion of a fanatical Maoist cult and that Mao's sanction for this was the desperate attempt of an ageing revolutionary to achieve immortality. Solomon (1971) sees Mao's encouragement of defiance against authority as a natural outcome of his own personality, illustrated by his youthful rebellion against his own father. Other studies have focused on the political infighting involved in the Cultural Revolution, showing how it was the outcome of a struggle between two 'lines' represented by Mao and Liu Shaoqi (Rice, 1972; Dittmer, 1974; Chang, 1975; Ahn, 1976).

It is clear, however, that the Cultural Revolution also has to be seen within the larger context of China's revolution in the twentieth century (Schram, 1973). Since the end of the nineteenth century, when Chinese intellectuals were coming to terms with China's weakness vis-à-vis the West, discussion had revolved around the central issue of how to make China wealthy, strong and united. It was argued that China should not only undertake political, military and economic reforms but should also transform cultural attitudes. Liang Qichao at the beginning of the twentieth century had urged the training of a new people (xinmin) which would be self-reliant, disciplined and public-spirited. May Fourth intellectuals after 1915 had condemned traditional attitudes and social customs, and advocated the inculcation of a democratic and scientific spirit among the people. For Mao, the Cultural Revolution was not just the means to remove his opponents within the party hierarchy. it was to be a full-scale attack on the very party itself by a new and politicized youth determined to root out all forms of revisionism and traditional thought that Mao was convinced had pervaded the party, bureaucracy and education system – the last, in particular, was a target of attack, with Liu Shaoqi being accused by Red Guards of having created a 'dual track system' that allowed a privileged few to take advantage of well-funded and urban-concentrated secondary and higher education while confining the majority of the school-age population to primary and inferior lower-secondary schools. In the process of 'struggle' Mao hoped that revolutionary idealism among the young would be revived.

Finally, it should be noted that the Cultural Revolution was accompanied by an increasingly shrill condemnation of both Soviet revisionism and American imperialism. It is significant, for example, that although American military involvement in Vietnam had steadily increased since 1964 so that by 1967 the United States was carrying out bombing raids on north Vietnam, Mao rejected any possibility that China and the Soviet Union might co-operate in assisting north Vietnam.

Retreat and the Rebuilding of the Party

Despite the premise laid down by the Sixteen Points that 'contradictions' among the people were to be resolved by reason and not coercion and that even 'anti-socialist rightists' should be allowed to repent, anarchy and violence became the order of the day. Party officials were publicly humiliated and paraded through the streets in dunces' caps; teachers, intellectuals and writers were physically attacked (and many of them were killed) and their books destroyed. Not only vestiges of the past, such as temples, were the target of attack; anyone professing an interest in western culture (for example in classical music) was also criticized and humiliated. Mao's thought, Red Guards claimed, would be used 'to turn the old world upside down, smash it to pieces, pulverize it, create chaos and make a tremendous mess, the bigger, the better' (Meisner, 1977, p. 315). Red Guards also often resorted to bitter fighting amongst themselves, each faction claiming to be the true upholders of Mao's thought (Hinton, 1972). This situation of virtual civil war has been graphically described in recent memoirs of former Red Guards (Liang Heng and Shapiro, 1983; Gao Yuan, 1986).

In February 1967 all party organization in Shanghai was dismantled, to be replaced by workers' organizations that called themselves the Shanghai Commune (Hunter, 1969). Mao was evidently beginning to feel that the breakdown of order had gone too far. He criticized the attempt to set up a commune in Shanghai as anarchy and referred to the necessity of creating revolutionary committees that would draw on representatives from mass organizations, the PLA and pro-Maoist cadres. Violence and chaos continued throughout 1967, however. The PLA itself came under attack by Red Guards and in August 1967 the British chancery in Beijing was attacked and burnt down.

In September 1967 Mao called on the PLA to restore order and the Red Guard movement was virtually ended. Thousands of Red Guards were sent to the countryside to take part in agricultural production. At the Party's Ninth Congress, in April 1969, priority was given to the task of party rebuilding. Ironically, a movement which had begun with an attack on all forms of authority ended with the military firmly in control. PLA representatives dominated the revolutionary committees while half of the central Committee membership was now from the PLA (Saich, 1981). Lin Biao himself had reached the apogee of his power, being officially proclaimed as Mao's successor.

At the Ninth Congress emphasis was also placed on reconstruction. The Cultural Revolution had brought chaos to the cities and had disrupted industrial production, although Meisner (1977, pp. 341–9) notes that certain beneficial changes had occurred in the countryside, such as the revival of small-scale industry and the shifting of medical and educational resources to rural areas. In the realm of education, schools and colleges were reopened, although entrance examinations were abolished and replaced by a system of recommendation that gave priority to ideological criteria. Students were also expected to undertake a compulsory period of manual labour before entering college.

In 1970 Mao sanctioned the subordination of revolutionary committees to newly formed party committees and called for the rehabilitation of pre-Cultural-Revolution cadres who had been purged during 1966–8. Lin Biao saw this as an attempt to reduce the influence of the PLA and hence as a threat to his power base. Lin also disagreed with Mao over the change in foreign policy that took place after 1970. Mao increasingly regarded Soviet 'hegemonism' as the greatest threat to world peace, especially after the Soviet invasion of Czechoslovakia in 1968 and border clashes in 1969 between Soviet and Chinese troops in the north-east. At the same time he began to put out feelers to the United States, whose intention to reduce its involvement in Vietnam seemed to make it less of a threat. In 1971 Secretary of State Kissinger visited China to prepare the way for President Nixon's official visit the following year. Lin opposed such developments, arguing that opposition to the United States was more necessary than opposition to the Soviet Union (Yahuda, 1978, p. 221). Lin's conflict with Mao came to a head in September 1971 when, according to later Chinese reports, he attempted to engineer a coup and assassinate Mao. The attempt failed and he was killed when the plane in which he was escaping crashed over Mongolia.

The years between 1971 and the death of Mao in 1976 witnessed a fierce tussle for direction of policy between the 'radicals' and 'pragmatists' (Brugger, 1981b). The radicals were led by Jiang Qing and her supporters Wang Hongwen (a former Shanghai factory worker), Zhang Chunqiao (former secretary of the Shanghai party committee) and Yao Wenyuan. All four, subsequently to be known as the 'Gang of Four' when they were purged in 1976, had been elected to the Politburo at the Tenth Party Congress in 1973. The pragmatists were led by the premier, Zhou Enlai, who had emerged unscathed from the Cultural Revolution despite Red Guard criticisms of him in 1967. In 1973 Zhou was able to use his influence to have

Deng Xiaoping rehabilitated, and he was appointed first vice-premier as well as a member of the Politburo Standing Committee.

Jiang Qing and her supporters frequently took issue with the policies of Zhou and Deng, which they saw as a deviation from the ideals of the Cultural Revolution. In particular, they criticized the policy of rehabilitating party cadres purged during the Cultural Revolution; Zhou's emphasis on economic and scientific development at the expense of ideology, illustrated by his long-term strategy of the Four Modernizations (agriculture, industry, national defence, science and technology) which he outlined at the Fourth National People's Congress in January 1975; and the reintroduction of university entrance examinations emphasizing academic criteria. Also, in line with China's opening to the world after the diplomatic isolation of the Cultural Revolution period, Zhou and Deng implemented an economic strategy that favoured export-led growth (consisting primarily of raw materials) and the importation of technology from the capitalist world. The radicals saw this as a betrayal of the hallowed concept of self-reliance.

The radicals were to achieve a partial victory in early 1976 when they prevented Deng from assuming the premiership after Zhou Enlai's death in January. Instead the post went to Hua Guofeng, minister of public security and former party boss in Hunan. In April 1976 Deng was accused of encouraging the Tian'anmen Riots, when thousands of Beijing citizens had angrily protested against the removal of wreaths that had been laid down in Tian'anmen Square in memory of Zhou Enlai. Deng was once again dismissed from his posts. Victory for the radicals, however, was short-lived.

Mao's death in September 1976, after a long illness of over a year during which he had played no significant part in policy-making, marked the end of an era in modern Chinese history. His legacy, however was an ambivalent one. He had forged a revolutionary strategy that had brought the CCP to power and resulted in the establishment of the People's Republic. After decades of internal chaos, disunity and civil war, and a century of imperialist exploitation and interference, China was once again a truly independent and unified nation state. In Mao's words, China 'had at last stood up'. Yet from the mid-1950s Mao had increasingly set himself above the party, convinced that his ideas alone embodied the true socialist vision. The logical outcome of this was his launching of the Cultural Revolution, which was a full-scale attack on the party itself. In the process a Maoist personality cult of grotesque proportions was created. Although Mao hoped to create a new revolutionary society, the Cultural Revolution brought violence and chaos to the cities and untold misery to thousands of intellectuals, writers and artists accused of being revisionist.

Mao was succeeded as chairman of the Central Committee by Hua Guofeng, who also retained the post of prime minister. The radicals evidently hoped that Hua would be a mere figurehead, allowing them to control policy, but, being in a minority in the Politburo, their position was always vulnerable. Barely one month later Hua had succeeded, with the support of the military, in having the Gang of Four arrested on charges of attempting a coup. By July 1977 Deng Xiaoping had been restored to his posts, as well as being appointed vice-chairman. The stage was now set for a radical change in direction.

Conclusion

Since Mao's death there have been significant changes in agricultural, education and population policy, some of which hark back to the early 1960s (Gardner, 1982; Hsü, 1983b; Bastid, 1984; Wong, 1984). In foreign policy Mao's successors have gone further in their 'open door policy' than Mao would have welcomed (Yahuda, 1983). In the realm of ideology and party organization, also, there have been changes. Mao's role in the Chinese revolution has been reinterpreted to take account of the 'ten bad years' (1966–76) of the Cultural Revolution and has resulted in a certain 'demythologizing' of his thought. At the same time, party leaders have called for 'socialist legalism' which would enjoin the party to conduct its activities 'within the limits permitted by the Constitution and the laws of the state' (Tsou, 1986, p. 308). Lifelong tenure, special privileges for cadres and excessive centralization of power have been condemned. At the same time, however, party leaders have consistently remained sensitive to any threat that might undermine party control, which has led to periodic campaigns against 'bourgeois liberalism'.

At the Third Plenum of the Eleventh Central Committee in December 1978 Deng Xiaoping raised the slogan of 'seeking truth from facts', which signalled the first steps in the evaluation of Mao's role and thought. During the winter of 1978 and spring of 1979 wall posters appeared in Beijing criticizing the excesses of the Cultural Revolution and advocating party reform. A former Red Guard activist, Wei Jingsheng, even argued that 'democracy' should be the Fifth Modernization (Nathan, 1985). Although the party abruptly clamped down on the Democracy Wall Movement in March 1979 when criticisms threatened to undermine party control (reminiscent of the Hundred Flowers campaign), the question of Mao's role in the Cultural Revolution still had to be confronted. When the Gang of Four were put on trial in 1980, accused of persecuting millions of people during the Cultural Revolution, Jiang Qing insisted that she and her associates had only been following Mao's directives. The Gang of Four were sentenced to long terms of imprisonment, but the dilemma remained.

The question was finally resolved at the Sixth Plenary Session of

78

the Eleventh Central Committee in June 1981. It was at this plenary session that Deng Xiaoping succeeded in having his protégé, Hu Yaobang, who was then party general secretary, succeed Hua Guofeng as party chairman (Hua had already had to give up the post of premier to another Deng supporter, Zhao Ziyang, in 1980). The Plenary Session adopted the 'resolution on Certain Questions in the History of the People's Republic', which, while recognizing Mao's great achievements as a revolutionary and leader of the CCP until the mid-1950s, noted that from 1955 onwards he committed 'errors' as a result of being out of touch with the needs and desires of the masses. This inevitably led to the 'ten bad years' of the Cultural Revolution and the fostering of a personality cult. The resolution made clear, however, that Mao's contributions outweighed his mistakes and that his thought (now defined as the 'crystallization of the *collective* wisdom of the party') would remain the party's guide to action. It could not have been otherwise. At a time when there was widespread cynicism about the party and even questioning of the viability of socialism itself, what the party press called a 'crisis of faith' (*xinyang weiji*), Mao could not be jettisoned. This 'crisis of faith' particularly affected those in their late twenties and early thirties, many of whom were former Red Guard activists who felt that they had been cynically manipulated and then rejected by the party.

In line with the emphasis on economic development there have been significant changes in agriculture. The individual peasant household, rather than the production team, became the unit of production with the adoption of the 'responsibility system' in 1980. Households could now sign contracts with, and lease land from, production teams. All investment and production decisions are made by the household and, after meeting its obligations to the state, it can dispose of its products in a greatly enlarged private sector. This has led to a rise in rural incomes but is by no means a uniform development since farming conditions and climate vary greatly from one region to another. The result of such agricultural reforms, however, has been the virtual dismantling of the commune.

In direct opposition to Maoist beliefs, which saw China's huge population as a positive advantage, the party now actively promotes birth control. In 1981 a State Family Planning Commission was established and laid down the norm that families were only to have one child in the hope that the population could be kept to 1.2 billion by the turn of the century (currently, the population is estimated to be 1 billion). Penalties are imposed on families if they have more than one child, for example the taking away of educational or medical benefits. Although the party's policy has met with success in the urban areas, there is widespread opposition in the countryside, where the persistence of traditional attitudes means that families attribute crucial importance to having sons so that the family line can be continued. Ironically, also, the party's agricultural reforms, by increasing the potential to raise rural incomes, indirectly encourage peasant families to have more sons in order to provide more labour for the family farm.

In education, also, there have been changes, although, like the agricultural reforms, they simply continue the process begun in the early 1960s. The stress is now on the *economic* role of education and priority is placed on the training of a scientific and technological elite in selective colleges and universities. Standardized national examinations have been restored and full four-year university courses introduced. These higher education institutions, known as 'keypoint' (*zhongdian*) colleges, are provided with students from a parallel network of 'keypoint' secondary schools, all of which are located in the urban areas. In fact, there has been a return to the 'dual track system' which Red Guards accused Liu Shaoqi of promoting in the early 1960s. The cultural segregation between town and countryside, which Mao had so often condemned, has not been ended.

Finally, the new Chinese leadership has promoted a vigorous open door policy and has been willing to go much further than merely importing technology from the West, which Mao countenanced during his last years. In 1979 a law on joint Sino-foreign ventures was passed (many of the new hotels in Beijing and elsewhere are joint ventures) and in 1980 the first Special Economic Zones were created in Guangdong and Fujian provinces where foreign investment was invited and Chinese labour could be hired. Thousands of students have been sent to the United States and Europe to study not only science and technology but also business management techniques. Relations with the United States were normalized in 1979, although this has not prevented Beijing from criticizing aspects of American foreign policy or from reopening a limited dialogue with the Soviet Union.

These changes have all been implemented under the guiding influence of Deng Xiaoping, but his position is not unassailable and he has constantly to take into account the criticisms of more conservative colleagues who argue that the economic reforms, in particular, threaten to undermine socialism because such reforms encourage greed and corruption. Deng himself is also determined that the economic reforms should not in any way threaten the party's leadership role and is particularly sensitive to the possible links between intellectual influences from outside and demands for more democracy in China. Thus in 1983 and recently, campaigns have been launched to combat 'spiritual pollution' (i.e. 'decadent bourgeois ideology') and 'bourgeois liberalism'. The problem that confronted Chinese officials in the late nineteenth century – how to import western technology without endangering the Confucian tradition – continues to plague Deng and his supporters, in the sense that they want to develop the economy with the assistance of outside technology and financial involvement but are anxious to prevent any undermining of party control that foreign cultural influences might bring about. This is the crucial issue which has to be resolved as China approaches the end of the twentieth century.

References and Further Reading

Ahn, B. J. 1976: *Chinese Politics and the Cultural Revolution*. Seattle.
Alitto, G. 1979: *The Last Confucian: Liang Shuming and the Chinese Dilemma of Modernity*. Berkeley.
Andors, P. 1983: *The Unfinished Liberation of Chinese Women 1949–1980*. Indiana.
Bastid, M. 1984: 'Chinese Educational Policies in the 1980s and Economic Development'. *China Quarterly*, vol. 98, pp. 189–219.
Baum, R. 1975: *Prelude to Revolution*. New York.
Bedeski, R. 1981: *State Building in Modern China*. Berkeley.
Bergère, M.C. 1983: 'The Chinese Bourgeoisie 1911–1937', in J. Fairbank (ed.), *The Cambridge History of China*, vol. 12. Cambridge.
Bernal, M. 1976: *Chinese Socialism to 1907*. Ithaca.
Bernstein, T. 1977: *Up to the Mountains and Down to the Villages*. New Haven.
Bianco, L. 1971: *Origins of the Chinese Revolution 1915–1949*. Stanford.
Borg, D. 1947: *American Policy and the Chinese Revolution 1925–1928*. New York.
Borg, D. 1964: *The United States and the Far Eastern Crisis of 1933–1938*. Cambridge, Mass.
Borthwick, S. 1983: *Education and Social Change in China*. Stanford.
Boyle, J. 1972: *China and Japan at War 1937–1945*. Stanford.
Brandt, C. 1958: *Stalin's Failure in China 1924–1927*. Cambridge, Mass.
Brugger, B. 1981a: *China: Liberation and Transformation 1942–1962*. London.
Brugger, B. 1981b: *China: Radicalism to Revolution 1962–1979*. London.
Bunker, G. 1971: *The Peace Conspiracy: Wang Ching-wei and the China War 1937–1941*. Cambridge, Mass.
Chan, A. 1982: *Arming the Chinese: The Western Armaments Trade in Warlord China*. Vancouver.
Chang, M. 1986: *The Chinese Blue Shirt Society*. Berkeley.
Chang, P. 1975: *Power and Policy in China*. Pennsylvania.
Ch'en, J. 1961: *Yuan Shih-k'ai*. London.
Ch'en, J. 1965: *Mao and the Chinese Revolution*. Oxford.
Chen, J. 1971: *The May Fourth Movement in Shanghai*. Leiden.
Chen T. 1974: *The Maoist Educational Revolution*. New York.
Chen, T. 1981: *Chinese Education Since Mao*. New York.
Chesneaux, J. 1968: *The Chinese Labour Movement*. Stanford.
Ch'i, Hsi-sheng. 1976: *Warlord Politics in China 1916–1928*. Stanford.
Ch'i, Hsi-sheng. 1982: *Nationalist China at War*. Michigan.
Chi, M. 1970: *China Diplomacy 1914–1918*. Cambridge, Mass.
Chow, Tse-tsung. 1960: *The May Fourth Movement*. Cambridge, Mass.

Clifford,, P. 1979: *Shanghai, 1925: Urban Nationalism and the Defence of Foreign Privilege*. Michigan.

Coble, P. 1980: *The Shanghai Capitalists and the Nationalist Government*. Cambridge, Mass.

Cochran, S. and Hsieh, A. (trs and eds) 1983: *One Day in China: May 21 1936*. New Haven.

Compton, B. (ed.) 1966: *Mao's China: Party Reform Documents 1942–1944*. Seattle.

Crowley, J. 1966: *Japan's Quest for Autonomy*. Princeton.

Dittmer, L. 1974: *Liu Shao-ch'i and the Chinese Cultural Revolution*. Berkeley.

Duiker, W. 1977: *Ts'ai Yuan-p'ei: Educator of Modern China*. Pennsylvania.

Eastman, L. 1974: *The Abortive Revolution*. Cambridge, Mass.

Eastman, L. 1980: 'Facets of an Ambivalent Relationship: Smuggling, Puppets, and Atrocities during the War 1937–1945', in A. Iriye (ed.), *The Chinese and the Japanese*. Princeton.

Eastman, L. 1984: *Seeds of Destruction: Nationalist China in War and Revolution 1937–1949*. Stanford.

Esherick, J. 1976: *Reform and Revolution in China: The 1911 Revolution in Hunan and Hubei*. Berkeley.

Feigon, L. 1983: *Chen Duxiu*. Princeton.

Feuerwerker, A. 1968: *The Chinese Economy 1912–1949*. Michigan.

Feuerwerker, A. 1983a: 'Economic Trends 1912–1949', in J. Fairbank (ed.), *The Cambridge History of China*, vol. 12. Cambridge.

Feuerwerker, A. 1983b: 'The Foreign Presence in China', in J. Fairbank (ed.), *The Cambridge History of China*, vol. 12. Cambridge.

Fewsmith, J. 1984: *Party, State and Local Elites in Republican China*. Hawaii.

Fincher, J. 1968: 'Political Provincialism and the National Revolution', in M. Wright (ed.), *China in Revolution: The First Phase 1900–1913*. New Haven.

Fincher, J. 1981: *Chinese Democracy*. New York.

Friedman, E. 1974: *Backward Toward Revolution: The Chinese Revolutionary Party*. Berkeley.

Fung, E. 1980: *The Military Dimension of the Chinese Revolution*. Vancouver.

Galbiati, F. 1985: *P'eng P'ai and the Hai-lu-Feng Soviet*. Stanford.

Gao Yuan, 1986: *Born Red*. Stanford.

Gardner, J. 1982: *Chinese Politics and the Succession to Mao*. London.

Gasster, M. 1969: *Chinese Intellectuals and the Revolution of 1911*. Seattle.

Gaulton, R. 1981: 'Political Mobilization in Shanghai 1949–1951', in C. Howe (ed.), *Shanghai: Revolution and Development in an Asian Metropolis*. Cambridge.

Gernet, J. 1982: *A History of Chinese Civilization*. Cambridge.

Gillin, D. 1964: 'Peasant Nationalism and Communist Power'. *Journal of Asian Studies*, vol. 23, pp. 269–89.

Gillin, D. 1967: *Warlord: Yen Hsi-shan in Shansi Province 1911–1949*. Princeton.

Gittings, J. 1967: *The Role of the Chinese Army*. New York.

Gittings, J. 1968: *A Survey of the Sino-Soviet Dispute*. Oxford.

Gittings, J. 1974: *The World and China 1922–1972*. London.

Goldman, M. 1973: 'The Chinese Communist Party's Cultural Revolution of 1962–1964', in C. Johnson (ed.), *Ideology and Politics in Contemporary China*. Seattle.

Goldman, M. 1981: *China's Intellectuals: Advice and Dissent*. Cambridge, Mass.

Greider, J. 1970: *Hu Shih and the Chinese Renaissance*. Cambridge, Mass.

Greider, J. 1981: *Intellectuals and the State in Modern China*. New York.

Guillermaz, J. 1972: *A History of the Chinese Communist Party 1921–1949*. New York.

Harding, H. 1981: *Organizing China: The Problem of Bureaucracy 1949–1976*. Stanford.
Harrison, J. 1972: *The Long March to Power*. New York.
Hinton, W. 1966: *Fanshen*. New York.
Hinton, W. 1972: *The Hundred Day War: The Cultural Revolution at Tsinghua University*. New York.
Ho, Ping-ti. 1959: *Studies on the Population of China 1368–1953*. Cambridge, Mass.
Hofheinz, R. 1977: *The Broken Wave: The Chinese Communist Peasant Movement 1920–1928*. Cambridge, Mass.
Hsü, I. 1975: *The Rise of Modern China*. New York.
Hsü, I. 1983a: *The Rise of Modern China*. 3rd rev. edn. New York.
Hsü, I. 1983b: *China Without Mao*. New York.
Hucker, C. 1975: *China's Imperial Past*. London.
Hunter, N. 1969: *Shanghai Journal: An Eyewitness Account of the Cultural Revolution*. New York.
Ichiko, Chuzo. 1980: 'Political and Institutional Reform 1901–1911', in J. Fairbank (ed.), *The Cambridge History of China,*, vol. 11. Cambridge.
Iriye, A. 1965: *After Imperialism: The Search for a New Order in the Far East 1921–1931*. Cambridge, Mass.
Iriye, A. 1967: *Across the Pacific: An Inner History of American–East Asian Relations*. New York.
Iriye, A. 1972: *Pacific Estrangement*. Cambridge, Mass.
Iröns, N. 1983: *The Last Emperor*. London.
Isräel, J. and Klein, D. 1976: *Rebels and Bureaucrats*. Berkeley.
Isaacs, H. 1961: *The Tragedy of the Chinese Revolution*. Stanford.
Jacobs, D. 1981: *Borodin: Stalin's Man in China*. Cambridge, Mass.
Jansen, M. 1954: *Sun Yat-sen and the Japanese*. Cambridge, Mass.
Jansen, M. 1972: *Japan and China: From War to Peace 1894–1972*. Chicago.
Jansen, M. 1980: 'The Japanese and the Chinese Revolution of 1911', in J. Fairbank (ed.), *The Cambridge History of China*, vol. 11. Cambridge.
Jansen, M. 1984: 'Japanese Imperialism: Late Meiji Perspectives', in R. Myers and M. Peattie (eds), *The Japanese Colonial Empire 1894–1945*. Princeton.
Johnson, C. 1962: *Peasant Nationalism and Communist Power*. Stanford.
Johnson, K. 1983: *Women, the Family and Peasant Revolution in China*. Chicago.
Jordan, D. 1976: *The Northern Expedition*. Honolulu.
Kapp. R. 1973: *Szechuan and the Chinese Republic*. New Haven.
Kataoka, T. 1974: *Resistance and Revolution in China*. Berkeley.
Kim, S. 1973: *The Politics of Chinese Communism: Kiangsi under the Soviets*. Berkeley.
Kirby, W. 1984: *Germany and Republican China*. Stanford.
Kuhn, P. 1978: 'The Taiping Rebellion ,in J. Fairbank (ed.), *The Cambridge History of China*, vol. 10. Cambridge.
Kwong L. 1984: *A Mosaic of the Hundred Days*. Cambridge, Mass.
Lary, D. 1974: *Region and Nation: The Kwangsi Clique in Chinese Politics 1925–1937*. Cambridge.
Lary, D. 1985: *Warlord Soldiers*. Cambridge.
Lee, Chong-sik. 1983: *Revolutionary Struggle in Manchuria*. Berkeley.
Lee, Leo Ou-fan (ed.) 1986: *Lu Hsun and his Legacy*. Berkeley.
Liang Heng and Shapiro, J. 1983: *Son of the Revolution*. New York.
Lieberthal, K. 1980: *Revolution and Tradition in Tientsin 1949–1952*. Stanford.
Liew, K. 1971: *Struggle for Democracy: Sung Chiao-jen and the 1911 Revolution*. Berkeley.
Lin, Yu-sheng. 1979: *The Crisis of Chinese Consciousness*. Madison.

Lifton, R. 1968: *Revolutionary Immortality*. New York.
Louis, W. 1971: *British Strategy in the Far East 1919–1939*. London.
Lyell, W. 1976: *Lu Xun's Vision of Reality*. Berkeley.
MacDonald, A. 1978: *The Urban Origins of Rural Revolution*. Berkeley.
MacFarquhar, R. (ed.) 1960: *The Hundred Flowers Campaign and the Chinese Intellectuals*. New York.
MacFarquhar, R. 1974: *The Origins of the Cultural Revolution, vol. 1: Contradictions Among the People*. London.
MacFarquhar, R. 1983: *The Origins of the Cultural Revolution, vol. 2: The Great Leap Forward*. London.
MacKinnon, S. 1980: *Power and Politics in Late Imperial China: Yuan Shikai in Beijing and Tianjin 1901–1908*. Berkeley.
Mancall, M. 1984: *China at the Center*. New York.
Mann Jones, S. and Kuhn, P. 1978: 'Dynastic decline and the roots of rebellion', in J. Fairbank (ed.), *The Cambridge History of China*, vol. 10. Cambridge.
Marks, R. 1984: *Rural Revolution in South China*. Madison.
McCormack, G. 1977: *Chiang Tso-lin in North-East China 1911–1928*. Stanford.
Meisner, M. 1967: *Li Ta-chao and the Origins of Chinese Marxism*. Cambridge, Mass.
Meisner, M. 1977: *Mao's China*. New York.
Moore, B. 1966: *Social Origins of Dictatorship and Democracy*. Boston.
Morton, W. 1980: *Tanaka Giichi and Japan's China Policy*. Folkestone.
Nathan, A. 1976: *Peking Politics 1918–1923*. Berkeley.
Nathan, A. 1985: *Chinese Democracy*. New York.
Nee, V. 1969: *The Cultural Revolution at Peking University*. New York.
Nobuya, B. 1972: *Japanese Diplomacy in a Dilemma*. Vancouver.
North, R. 1953: *Moscow and Chinese Communists*. Stanford.
Ogata, S. 1964: *Defiance in Manchuria*. Berkeley.
Peattie, M. 1975: *Ishiwara Kanji and Japan's Confrontation with the West*. Princeton.
Pepper, S. 1978: *Civil War in China*. Berkeley.
Price, R. 1970: *Education in Communist China*. London.
Price, R. 1977: *Marx and Education in Russia and China*. London.
Pye, L. 1971: *Warlord Politics*. New York.
Reardon-Anderson, J. 1980: *Yenan and the Great Powers*. New York.
Rhoads, E. 1975: *China's Republican Revolution: The Case of Kwangtung 1895–1913*. Cambridge, Mass.
Rice, E. 1972: *Mao's Way*. Berkeley.
Rue, J. 1966: *Mao Tse-tung in Opposition 1927–1935*. Stanford.
Saich, T. 1981: *China: Politics and Government*. New York.
Schaller, M. 1979: *The US Crusade in China 1938–1945*. New York.
Schiffrin, H. 1968: *Sun Yat-sen and the Origins of the Chinese Revolution*. Berkeley.
Schram, S. 1963: *The Political Thought of Mao Tse-tung*. New York.
Schram, S. 1966: *Mao Tse-tung*. Harmondsworth.
Schram, S. 1973: 'The Cultural Revolution: An Historical Introduction', in S. Schram (ed.), *Authority, Participation and Cultural Change in China*. Cambridge.
Schram, S. (ed.) 1974: *Mao Tse-tung Unrehearsed*. Harmondsworth.
Schurmann, F. 1968: *Ideology and Organization in Communist China*. Berkeley.
Schwarcz, V. 1986: *The Chinese Enlightenment*. Berkeley.
Schwartz, B. 1979: *Chinese Communism and the Rise of Mao*. Cambridge, Mass.
Seagrave, S. 1985: *The Soong Dynasty*. London.
Selden, M. 1971: *The Yenan Way in Revolutionary China*. Cambridge, Mass.
Shaffer, L. 1982: *Mao and the Workers*. New York.

Sheridan, J. 1966: *Chinese Warlord: The Career of Feng Yu-hsiang*. Stanford.

Sheridan, J. 1977: *China in Disintegration*. New York.

Sheridan, J. 1983: 'The Warlord Era: Politics and Militarism under the Peking Government 1916–1928', in J. Fairbank (ed.), *The Cambridge History of China*, vol. 12. Cambridge.

Shue, V. 1980: *Peasant China in Transition*. Berkeley.

Shum, K. 1985: 'The Chinese Communist Party's Strategy for Galvanising Popular Support 1930–1945', in D. Pong and E. Fung (eds), *Ideal and Reality: Social and Political Change in Modern China 1860–1949*. Lanham.

Solomon, R. 1971: *Mao's Revolution and the Chinese Political Culture*. Berkeley.

Spence, J. 1981: *The Gate of Heavenly Peace: The Chinese and their Revolution 1895–1980*. New York.

Stacy, J. 1983: *Patriarchy and Socialist Revolution in China*. Berkeley.

Storry, R. 1979: *Japan and the Decline of the West in Asia 1894–1943*. London.

Summerskill, M. 1982: *China on the Western Front*. London.

Sutton, D. 1980: *Provincial Militarism and the Chinese Republic*. Ann Arbor.

Thaxton, R. 1983: *China Turned Rightside Up*. New Haven.

Thorne, C. 1972: *The Limits of Foreign Policy: The West, the League, and the Far Eastern Crisis 1931–1933*. London.

Thornton, R. 1969: *The Comintern and the Chinese Communists 1928–1931*. Seattle.

Thornton, R. 1973: *China: The Struggle for Power 1917–1972*. Bloomington.

Townsend, J. 1967: *Political Participation in Communist China*. Berkeley.

Tsou, Tang. 1986: *The Cultural Revolution and Post-Mao Reforms*. Chicago.

Tuchman, B. 1970: *Sand Against the Wind: Stilwell and the American Experience in China*. London.

Tucker, N. 1983: *Patterns in the Dust: Chinese–American relations and the Recognition Controversy 1949–1950*. New York.

Vogel, E. 1969: *Canton under Communism*. New York.

Wakeman, F. 1975: *The Fall of Imperial China*. New York.

Waller, D. 1973: *The Kiangsi Soviet Republic*. Berkeley.

Whiting, A. 1954: *Soviet Policies in China 1917–1924*. New York.

Whiting, A. 1960: *China Crosses the Yalu: The Decision to Enter the Korean War*. New York.

Wilbur, M. 1968: 'Military Separatism and the Process of Re-unification under the Nationalist Regime', in Ho Ping-ti and Tang Tsou (eds), *China in Crisis*, vol. 1. Chicago.

Wilbur, M. 1976: *Sun Yat-sen: Frustrated Patriot*. New York.

Wilbur,, M. 1983: 'The Nationalist Revolution: From Canton to Peking 1923–1928', in J. Fairbank (ed.), *The Cambridge History of China*. vol. 12. Cambridge.

Womack, B. 1982: *The Foundations of Mao Zedong's Political Thought 1917–1935*. Honolulu.

Wong, J. 1973: *Land Reform in the People's Republic of China*. New York.

Wong, Sui-lun. 1984: 'Consequences of China's New Population Policy'. *China Quarterly*, vol. 98, pp. 220–40.

Wou,. O. 1978: *Militarism in Modern China: The Career of Wu P'ei-fu 1916–1939*. Dawson.

Wright, M. 1968: 'Introduction: The Rising Tide of Change', in M. Wright (ed.), *China in Revolution: The First Phase 1900–1913*. New Haven.

Wu, Tian-wei. 1976 *The Sian Incident*. Ann Arbor.

Wylie, R. 1980: *The Emergence of Maoism*. Stanford.

Yahuda, M. 1978: *China's Role in World Affairs*. 'London.

Yahuda, M. 1983: *Towards the End of Isolationism*. London.

Yang, C. 1959: *Chinese Communist Society: The Family and the Village*. Cambridge, Mass.

Young, E. 1968: 'Yuan Shih-k'ai's Rise to the Presidency', in M. Wright (ed.), *China in Revolution: The First Phase 1900–1913*. New Haven.

Young, E. 1970: 'Nationalism, Reform and Republican Revolution: China in the Early Twentieth Century', in J. Crowley (ed.), *Modern East Asia: Essays in Interpretation*. New York.

Young, E. 1976: 'The Hung-Hsien Emperor as a Modernizing Conservative', in C. Furth (ed.), *The Limits of Change*. Cambridge, Mass.

Young, E. 1977: *The Presidency of Yuan Shih-k'ai*. Ann Arbor.

Young, E. 1983: 'Politics in the Aftermath of Revolution: The Era of Yuan Shih-k'ai 1912–1916', in J. Fairbank (ed.), *The Cambridge History of China*, vol. 12. Cambridge.

Yu, G. 1966: *Party Politics in Republican China*. Berkeley.

Zagoria,D. 1962: *The Sino-Soviet Conflict 1956–1961*. Princeton.

Index